Acknowledgments

I want to thank all the children that God has placed in my life over these many years to love and teach. You have taught me more than I could have ever taught you. First of all, I would like to thank my own children, who are grown and active in teaching, each in his or her own way. You have done more to shape my heart than all the books and classes ever could. I love you Angela, Christopher, Damon and Kathy with all my heart.

I thank my husband, Paul, who patiently endured my writing of another book. Thank you for your faithfulness and support.

Thank you, Legacy Board of Directors, for making all of my school dreams not only come true but be more than I could ever dream.

Thank you, Legacy Christian Academy teachers and administrators, who truly teach with heart and love these students from pre-K to seniors with your passion for Jesus Christ. Thank you for discipling His children to be all they can be for the cause of Christ.

Thank you, dear friend and our lower school principal, Joyce Myers, for your friendship and support during the back surgeries I had while writing this book. We share our love for Christ, children, and books, and I thank you for sharing your life experience as a missionary and minister to children.

Thank you, Sandy Stockton and Emily Herrick, for retyping this book when lightning hit our home and took with it my computer and this manuscript.

And thank you, dear Christina Wallace, who was editor extraordinaire. You brought life and love to the process and working with you is a joy.

Table of Contents

Introduction 5

1. Cherishing and Challenging 7

2. Cherishing and Challenging Children
by Becoming a Teacher with HEART 13

3. Cherishing and Challenging Children
to Fit God's Design of Their Personalities 25

4. Cherishing and Challenging Children
to Fit God's Design of Their Learning Modalities 43

5. Cherishing and Challenging Children
to Fit God's Design of Their Learning Languages 57

6. Cherishing and Challenging Children
Through Multiple Intelligences and Faith Development 71

7. Cherishing and Challenging Children
to Fit God's Design of Their Brain Orientation 87

8. Cherishing and Challenging Children
by Enhancing and Enriching Your Classroom Environment . . . 103

9. Cherishing and Challenging Children
Through Appropriate Classroom Discipline 117

10. Cherishing and Challenging Children
Through Christlike Communication 141

11. Cherishing and Challenging Children
to Build Healthy Self-Esteem 155

12. Cherishing and Challenging Children
to Develop Responsibility 167

13. Cherishing and Challenging Children
to Make Meaningful Memories 177

14. Cherishing and Challenging Children
with the Power of Prayer 191

15. Cherishing and Challenging Children
by Using Curriculum with HEART 205

Bibliography 214

In the 80s I wrote several books that I believed represented different aspects of my life. I self-published two time organizers called *A Gift of Time;* one for busy moms and the other for schoolteachers. I wrote *Cherishing and Challenging Your Children* that I believed represented my heart as a mother. I also wrote *Becoming a Treasured Teacher,* which communicated my heart as a teacher, and *Once Upon a Time,* a book about who I am in Jesus Christ. I was surprised to discover that colleges and schools were using the book *Cherishing and Challenging Your Children* as a teacher-training book, especially within the circles of Early Childhood. Therefore, I wanted to rewrite it specifically as a teacher-training guide.

It is now 20 years later, and my dream is being realized. The Lord has taken me through many changes over the years, and I believe this book reflects much of the journey. When I wrote the other books, I had completed 2 years of teaching in public schools—one in a foreign country and 15 as a school principal of a private school. The Lord then brought me into the world of church education, an arena that I loved and in which I imagined I would retire. The Lord had other plans. He led me back into the world of school education and into training in classical education, learning styles, and brain development.

With God's grace I have had the blessing of founding five schools. My journey has led me to founding and serving as headmaster of Legacy Christian Academy, a Christian, classical school for students pre-K through 12th grade. I am deeply blessed with an excellent board of directors, faculty, staff, parents, and students, and a beautiful facility and campus. While these blessings reach beyond words, the passion that began my journey as a young person still remains at the core of everything.

I am completely in love with children of all ages. I often say: "It's all about Jesus, and it's all about investing in the lives of young people who are our future." Children always have and always will "float my boat," as the expression goes.

God is the author and ultimate creator of everything. If we look at a garden, we see that some plants need bright sun, while others require shade. Some require lots of water to bloom, and others require very little. We can apply this garden view to the students we teach.

Each child is completely unique and created for God's purpose. Some children want to lead, and others want to follow. Some children require lots of direction, while others do not. In His garden God creates each of us to be completely unique, in order to fulfill His mission in us. I marvel at the infinite creativity in each child. All children need to be cherished and challenged. As we become better equipped as teachers to understand and teach to the uniqueness of each child, we are able to fully equip him to be all that God has intended him to be. Thus, the more we learn to cherish, the better challengers we become.

After over 30 years of teaching children, I still stand in awe of the creator. The world has become incredibly complex, and sadly, more carnal. The corridors of childhood are precarious places. It is no longer safe to be a child, and the season of childhood innocence grows ever shorter. Who will be there for the children?

I pray that I will remain in the corridors for the children until the Lord calls me home. I praise God every day for the opportunity to love His precious children, to teach them, to encourage them, and to help them realize their God-given potential. It's not about me; it's all about Jesus, and it's all for the children. Won't you join me on the journey?

Teaching with Heart

Standard
PUBLISHING
Bringing The Word to Life™

Cincinnati, Ohio

Dedication

To my son Christopher David Capehart, who has dedicated his life to reaching and teaching young people for Jesus Christ. Thank you, Christopher, for teaching with HEART in every sense of the word.

Published by Standard Publishing, Cincinnati, Ohio
www.standardpub.com

13 12 11 10 09 08 07 06   9 8 7 6 5 4 3 2

ISBN-13: 987-0-7847-1347-1
ISBN-10: 0-7847-1347-2

Edited by Christina Wallace
Cover design by Liz Malwitz
Interior design by Sandra Wimmer
Interior illustrations by Rusty Fletcher

Chapter 1

Cherishing and Challenging

A Teacher with HEART understands the importance of cherishing and challenging to the individuality of each child.

Scripture: "For you created my inmost being; you knit me together in my mother's womb. I praise you because I am fearfully and wonderfully made; your works are wonderful, I know that full well" (Psalm 139:13, 14).

Teaching Objective: To understand what it means to cherish and challenge each student that God has placed in our ministry.

When I was speaking in Denver, I had the opportunity to see a Colorado snowstorm firsthand. As I do so often, I found myself in awe of our creator. He could have easily made each snowflake the same. But He chose to make each one completely unique. What is His purpose? I believe it is to show us how much value He places upon the uniqueness of each of His creations. God delights in individuality. Why then do we try to get everyone to conform to one set way of doing things? Why do we try so often to produce the canned green beans mentality? Instead, we should strive for and rejoice with the "garden variety" that I believe our Heavenly Father created us to be for His kingdom.

What Does It Mean?

We can more effectively cherish the children God has given us to teach when we embrace their differences and recognize them as God-given. And we can challenge them more effectively when we learn the best ways to work in and through these differences. Since God has chosen us to teach these precious children, then He must be delighted to show us His way to wisely handle this unique gift. We must have an open, teachable spirit and be willing to be humbled, lest we tumble.

Cherishing means "to treat with love, treating with affection and tenderness; to hold dear" (Webster's Dictionary, 1928). Similar ideas include valuing, affirming, accepting, commending, and caring. As teachers we want to reflect the love of Jesus. We want to translate the unconditional love of Christ into the hearts of the students we teach. *Cherishing* is absolutely essential if we seek to model our example after the master teacher, Jesus Christ. Nothing will hinder our ministry and our message as much as a failure to cherish the children entrusted to our care.

Challenging is defined as "calling for full use of one's abilities or resources in a difficult but stimulating effort; absorbing; intriguing" (Webster's Dictionary, 1928). We may perceive it as stretching, presenting opportunities to grow, and assigning tasks aimed at further development. As teachers we want to challenge the students to be all they can be for Jesus and to do this within the context of the gifts and qualities with which He's so richly blessed each child. In this fallen world we are bombarded with declining morals and standards. It is critical that we challenge our students to a higher level of spiritual excellence.

> **As teachers we can translate the unconditional love of Christ into the hearts of the students we teach.**

Finding a Balance

Cherishing includes:
- Unconditional love (liking them when they do not seem so loveable)
- Identifying and affirming the best in each child
- Encouraging them through their individuality to be the best they can be
- Simply enjoying them for who they are because God created them

Over-cherishing and under-challenging:

The balance is critical. We have all experienced children in our classrooms who have been over cherished and under challenged. The result may be a child who:
- Is spoiled
- Seems overly sensitive
- Is self-centered
- Appears self-absorbed
- Cannot see beyond his own needs to the needs of others
- Wants and expects to get his own way

Challenging includes:
- Teaching to and through the God-given potential in each child
- Stretching their understanding of their own capabilities
- Keeping the bar high for our standards for holiness and respect as members of God's family
- Empowering them to be all they can be

Over-challenging and under-cherishing:

When a child is over challenged and under cherished, the result may be a child who seems:
- Afraid
- Insecure
- Extremely introverted
- Inappropriately extraverted
- Unable to apologize when wrong
- Drawn toward bullying tendencies

There are obvious dangers and pitfalls in the realm of learning to cherish and challenge children with balance. However, regardless of the possible snares along the way, teachers must learn to cherish and challenge to and through the God-designed individuality of each child.

God's Infinite Designs

> **Understanding personality patterns will help you become a better teacher and your students better learners.**

God continually reveals himself in all of creation and displays His infinite variety in ways that remind us that He is the master creator. We see the majesty of His mountains, the beauty of the seas, the glorious colors of the flowers that bloom in different seasons. He often hides the richness of oil in barren places. From the seemingly lifeless tree, He brings forth beautiful blossoms in the spring. At every corner of His creation we see infinite diversity and His creativity abounds.

There are obviously many ways that we can observe God's infinite design. As we study the patterns of how children develop in their personalities and temperaments, we can learn to utilize their differences to help them learn. We become better teachers and, in the process, help them become better learners. There are volumes written today on the various names for their individual differences and characteristics. It can be overwhelming, so I have selected a few of these areas that will be especially helpful to study in our pursuit of learning to correctly cherish and challenge the children we teach. My purpose in viewing these differences is to help you more effectively *cherish* the way God made children and then to provide practical ways to challenge them to be all that God intended.

We are better able to cherish and challenge children when we can embrace their differences and acknowledge our creator's sovereign purpose in making each child the way He has. That's easy to say when we have an easy child to teach. It is much more difficult to say when God presents you with a very diverse and difficult classroom of students. It's a joy to see God's design in the *easy* children, but what about those *difficult* children? Where is God's beautiful design now? Since we know God wasn't dozing off when He created some children, we trust in His infinite purpose as the master designer.

The purpose of this book is two-fold. My aim is to help teachers understand and cherish the differences in each unique child, and also to provide teachers with positive methods of appropriately challenging children to understand and to make the best use of their individuality for God's kingdom.

How to Cherish and Challenge in the Classroom

Answer the following questions to explore ways you can effectively cherish and challenge the students you teach.

1. List seven ways that you can be a teacher who truly cherishes your students.

-
-
-
-
-
-
-

2. What are seven ways you can effectively challenge the children in your classroom?

-
-
-
-
-
-
-

3. What are three ways you have observed the infinite designs of our Heavenly Father?

-
-
-

4. List three ways His designs are evidenced in the children you teach?

-
-
-

5. What have you observed in the children you teach that shows that they are appropriately cherished?

6. What about *over* cherished?

7. What have you observed in the children you teach that shows a positive amount of challenging?

8. What about *over* challenging?

9. What changes do you hope to see in the children that you teach through the coming year that reflect progress in the areas of appropriate cherishing and challenging?

Cherishing and Challenging

Defining Cherishing and Challenging

Fill in the appropriate spaces below. Then review the definitions and descriptions of how to appropriately cherish and challenge your students.

I. _____ means to "treat with love, treating with affection and tenderness; to hold dear."
- Similar ideas include valuing, affirming, accepting, commending, and caring.
- In cherishing, teachers aim to reflect the love of Jesus.
- Translate the unconditional love of Jesus into the hearts of the students you teach.

II. _____ is defined as "calling for full use of one's abilities or resources in a difficult but stimulating effort; absorbing; intriguing."
- Similar ideas include stretching, presenting opportunities to grow, and assigning tasks aimed at further development.
- In challenging, we move students to be all they can be for Jesus within the context of the gifts and qualities with which He has blessed them.
- Due to the declining morals and standards in today's society, it is critical that we challenge our students to a higher level of spiritual excellence.

III. Appropriate _____ includes:
- Offering unconditional love (_____ them when they don't seem so _____)
- Identifying and affirming the best in each child
- Encouraging them through their individuality to be the best they can be
- Simply enjoying them for who they are, because God created them

IV. Over-_____ can lead to children who:
- Are spoiled
- Seem overly sensitive
- Are self-centered
- Are self-absorbed
- Cannot see beyond their own needs to the needs of others
- Want and expect to get their own way

V. Appropriate _____ includes:
- Teaching to and through the God-given potential in each child
- Stretching them to understand their own capabilities
- Keeping the bar high for out standards for _____ and _____
- Empowering them to be all they can be for Jesus

VI. Over-_____ can lead to children who:
- Are afraid
- Seem insecure
- Are extremely introverted
- May be inappropriately extraverted
- Are unable to apologize when wrong
- Show tendencies toward bullying

Chapter 2

Cherishing and Challenging Children by Becoming a Teacher with HEART

A Teacher with HEART understands the importance of modeling a holy life, maintaining a teachable spirit, teaching using age appropriate methods, remaining relevant to the culture, and staying true to the Bible in all things.

Scripture: "Whatever you do, work at it with all your heart, as working for the Lord, not for men, since you know that you will receive an inheritance from the Lord as a reward. It is the Lord Christ you are serving" (Colossians 3:23, 24).

Teaching Objective: To become a teacher with HEART.

Holy Lives Transformed by the Spirit

There is little that is sacred in our world anymore. We are submerged daily in a culture that does not recognize the importance of being set apart for the Lord and His purposes. We want children to embrace the incredible holiness of God in a fallen world that lives contrary to everything that is holy. We want children to learn to live holy lives dedicated to the Lord. But how do we help them do this? How do we train children to live holy lives in a world that is antithetical to holiness?

We must remember that without true regeneration, our teaching remains on the periphery. Without a personal relationship with Jesus Christ, our teaching does not transform lives. Only through Jesus can we receive the gift of the Holy Spirit. It is the call of Christ, combined with the power of the Holy Spirit, that cultivates a home in our hearts and lives for holiness. God gives us an amazing gift at the moment of salvation—the power of the Holy Spirit dwelling in us. We must be attentive to the danger of becoming desensitized to the infinite power of this gift to elevate us to higher levels of holiness in our personal lives and in our teaching.

You may have heard of the frog in the kettle paradigm. The harsh reality is that many of us have been impacted by it more than we realize. Just as the frog in the kettle is slowly heated to boiling, never realizing or sensing the danger, we are insidiously being changed by our culture. The entertainment-saturated media has brought a high need on the behalf of children and adults alike to be entertained at church.

If we want to cultivate holiness in the children we teach we must help them to experience it. I pray for children to experience holiness and worship in church, at school, and in their personal lives. I want them to purposely choose to be set apart from their culture and its ideas and to bring this changed mindset into their worship.

As a minister to children for eight years, I strove to place holiness at the focus of our worship times. I often felt counter to the culture. I want children to love coming to church. I love to make the children's ministry programs exciting and interesting but not at the cost of compromising worship. He is worthy of our worship, and inherent in that is holiness.

Perhaps I am old-fashioned in what I consider as giving one's best to God. I am old enough to remember when stores were not permitted to open on Sundays. This provided a natural motivation to focus on the Lord and family. Today, however, we'll often put sports at a higher level than church events. Ouch! As teachers

> We will struggle to teach children how to live holy lives if we are not making a concerted effort in our own.

of the Word, we must prayerfully examine the degree of holiness in our own lives, and how we are striving to be set apart and live counter to our culture, before we make efforts toward molding the character of the children we teach.

Character is contagious. Children can quickly discern if there is consistency between our talk and our walk. We will struggle to teach children how to live holy lives if we are not making a concerted effort in our own. How can we model holiness to those we teach? We do it through prayer, personal Bible study, worship, and surrounding ourselves with others who also seek to be set apart. We can help children learn to live holy lives by setting an example for them in every encounter. We can do this

1) in speech, "Do not let any unwholesome talk come out of your mouths, but only what is helpful for building others up according to their needs, that it may benefit those who listen" (Ephesians 4:29);

2) in life, "Live such good lives among the pagans that, though they accuse you of doing wrong, they may see your good deeds and glorify God" (1 Peter 2:12);

3) in love, "Jesus replied: 'Love the Lord your God with all your heart and with all your soul and with all your mind.' This is the first and greatest commandment. And the second is like it: 'Love your neighbor as yourself'" (Matthew 22:37-39);

4) in faith, "Now faith is being sure of what we hope for and certain of what we do not see" (Hebrews 11:1);

5) in purity, "Now we are children of God, and what we will be has not yet been made known. But we know that when he appears, we shall be like him, for we shall see him as he is. Everyone who has this hope in him purifies himself, just as he is pure" (1 John 3:2, 3).

If we focus on these five areas, we will be living holy lives that are set apart for the Lord and His purposes, thus encouraging our students to do the same through our example. Speaking without putting others down, living a life above reproach, loving God above all and others as ourselves, having faith in something we cannot see, and striving for purity as God's children are all counter to our culture's mindset. As teachers with HEART we must strive to lead holy lives and to encourage and teach our students to be set apart for the Lord.

Easy to Teach: Maintaining a Teachable Spirit

In order to teach with HEART, we must maintain a teachable spirit. What does this mean? It means being approachable, open to correction, willing to learn from others—even our students, and showing the same respect to others.

Approachable: It has been said that hurry is not of the devil, it is the devil. For me, I know this to be very true. When I am operating on a tight schedule with many looming deadlines, I find that I am not gracious when people approach me with problems and issues that they want answers and resolution to right away. Even if I try and smile, inwardly I am churning. But when I am not in the middle of major deadlines and meetings, I enjoy talking with a parent or teacher about an issue.

I have the incredible blessing of being a part of the extraordinary ministry of Stonebriar Church where Chuck Swindoll is the senior pastor. I watch Chuck during and between all three services and I stand in awe of his presence with people. He is the same transparent person in the pulpit as he is between each service. He is patient and totally focused on each person who approaches him. There are some pastors who may be different in the pulpit than they are in person—but not Chuck. He is the same loving, fun, real, authentic, and approachable person in the pulpit that he is in person. What a treasure to the body of Christ at large, and our church and family in particular.

My days are long. I often get to work before anyone arrives and stay after everyone leaves. Why? So that during the day I can be more approachable and accessible to the people that God has put on my schedule. Even at this very moment there is a parent waiting to see me because she saw my car in the parking lot and thought she could see me before the day begins. Inside I am churning, *This is my time, and I came here to get this done before the day begins at 7:00 A.M.,* but I know in my heart that it is on God's to-do list and not mine. I am praying to surrender my will. It is a daily journey. Some days I pass the test and other days I flunk, but I must persevere with a patient heart because ultimately, it is all about Him and His agenda and not my own.

God has taught me through my experiences with my own children that a teachable moment will not come back and that I need to live by God's to-do list and not my own. When we want children to talk and pour out their hearts, they usually do not. But when we are busy it seems like they want to talk for hours. I have learned to surrender the moment to God because children are more

> Being submissive means truly laying down the desire to always have my own way.

important than any project. The work will wait, but I may not get this very special divine appointment again. I don't feel that I always succeed in this area, but I work hard at it. This very issue keeps me on my knees. I want to always be approachable.

Open to correction: Being in ministry for 34 years has taught me that you often get credit for things that you didn't do and blamed for things you didn't do. In God's economy I figure it all balances out. But it does hurt when people misquote or misunderstand you. For many years I wanted to make the wrong right. God has taught me to be patient with people and trust Him to take care of things that I may not think are fair. Being submissive means truly laying down the desire to always have my own way. I pray every morning on the way to work to surrender my will to His.

God has also taught me to listen and to try to see things through the lens of His Holy Spirit. If someone is angry, I know now that there is usually hurt at the core of it. I listen for the hurt and reflect the feeling. With most issues, people just need to be heard. If they are upset with me and I truly listen to their hearts and the part that I truly need to hear, God gives me ears to hear. When I realize my part of this problem, I can respond with authenticity that I am truly sorry. Apologizing dissipates anger faster than anything.

Just this week there was a discipline issue with a student who was angry. I am older than my male high school administrators and I told them before the conference, "We are going to love this young man to wholeness. Anger is the only language he knows because of his home situation and if we respond to his anger with anger, we will lose." We prayed, listened, and sometime during the conference one of the administrators said to the student, "I am sorry for being defensive with your attitude and criticism." Immediately the young man's anger left. He just needed to be heard. At that moment that excellent administrator grew up 10 years. It takes a real man to say "I'm sorry," but those words heal.

Every day I pray to hold every thought, word, and deed captive to Christ (2 Corinthians 10:5) and to have the ears to hear what God is teaching me.

Willing to learn from others: As Christians, we are continually growing in our walk. That is the joy and beauty of sanctification. If we stop growing, we will become stagnant. Sometimes it is a child who leads us. When a student corrects me, or knows more than I do on a subject, I welcome it. I say, "I am so impressed that you know this, please share it with the class." Yes, sometimes it is embarrassing, but it is more important to be teachable. Even Jesus

Christ acknowledged how great children are. We need to be like little children—teachable, approachable and ever eager to learn and grow.

Showing the same respect to others: Approaching others with the same level of respect that we expect for ourselves honors them and helps enable them to maintain a teachable spirit. Having mutual respect in a relationship is essential if the relationship is to be healthy.

Part of teaching with HEART is to train students how to be respectful. You must model this for your students. When you need to talk with them, set up a time to meet and talk with them in private. If you need to interrupt them, say "Excuse me." When you call on them or ask them to do a task, remember to model good manners. Children learn far more from what we are than from what we say. As the teacher it is imperative that your heart be right in how you deal with your students, parents, and other teachers. Children are watching. What are you teaching?

When you make a mistake, and we all do, apologize. This models authenticity and a teachable spirit. You are teaching your students a life lesson: it is OK to make a mistake. Be real with your students because through your example, they learn to trust you. Show Jesus to them in every way—by your love, attitude, respect, transparency, and humility. It's not about us, it's all about Jesus.

Age-Appropriate Teaching Methods

How does a teacher with HEART create a learning climate that is conducive to cultivate the Christlike transformation she wants in her students? While inner transformation is the ultimate goal, sometimes it is easier to begin on the outside. Set up the learning environment so that it is appropriate to the ages of the students you teach. For example, a preschool environment needs to be set up with bright, colorful pictures from the Bible on the eye level of the students. The furniture needs to be appropriate for the ages of the children. An elementary classroom may have biblical time lines and maps that invite interest and engage the learner. A high school room may have posters that challenge the students and stimulate discussions. The learning environment needs to say "Come on in, you will love what we are learning today!"

The classroom needs to be learner-centered while at the same time communicating that the teacher is in charge. The teacher needs to be attentive and maintain classroom management while at the same time teaching and engaging the learners. Whew! That is a complex task! It involves a balance, order, and creativity.

> **Children learn far more from what we are than from what we say.**

Teacher-in-charge and learner-centered is a combination that I pray you will learn to develop as you learn to teach with HEART.

Communication must be clear and concise in an effort to remain age appropriate. Teach using words that your students can hear and understand. The language of learning is best spoken by teaching to each of the different learning styles. Finding ways to use visuals that are age appropriate, cultivate discussions in order to allow students to complete the learning cycle of hearing and talking, and provide opportunities to touch and to participate in the learning process will help you to actively engage your learners.

Our words need to build bridges to connect with our students. Connecting words are those that are encouraging, empowering, and engaging to the student. Words that create roadblocks are those that are critical, condescending, and contrived.

Relevant to the Culture

We must understand our culture in order to make our teaching relevant. We have to develop the strengths of our own convictions by asking ourselves where we stand on the complex issues that confront us on a daily basis.

Unfortunately we live in a culture that has become spiritually dumbed-down as well as numbed-up. We don't tend to flinch as much when we hear bad language. We may not be as repelled by the magazine covers confronting us as we stand in line at the grocery store. The pagan messages on television may even intrigue us rather than repel us. Perhaps each of us has become compromised in some way by our culture.

So how do we help our students become strong and live counter to their culture? Through authenticity. As we pray to become more pure, our lens becomes less foggy. God's Word must be the light to our paths, and yet the truth of living this reality may be a daily challenge for many of us at times. When we share with our students a struggle that we have faced during the week, they hear us because we are being real. They can relate to real struggles. They turn us off when we present a holier-than-thou attitude and merely preach to them. They hear our hearts when we share in the journey with them. We can then equip them as we have allowed the Lord to equip us.

Taking the time to understand the culture our students are products of, and to make our teaching relevant to their culture, requires a relationship with them. Our students may not see the relevance of our message until they know that we care and want to have a

Your students hear your heart when you share in the journey with them.

relationship with them. Love is truly spelled T-I-M-E. The time that we invest getting to know our students, asking about their interests and involving ourselves in their lives, will reap rich dividends in our teaching.

Mary Manz Simon helps us to understand the terms that define the world that our students live in today. She states that we must be aware of, and realistically understand, what terms like solo chill (previously: couch potato), viral marketing (which is word of mouse rather than word of mouth), and yogurt sites (which are meeting places for kids with active cultures that attract tweens and teens regardless of economic conditions) mean. If we want to reach children, we must go where they are and speak in words they can truly understand.

We can use the tools of media as part of our lessons. But we must take time to be familiar with what our students are being exposed to in the media if we are to counter it. We must understand their cultural language if we want to truly connect with them. This takes time. We don't have to be like them but we must show that we love them by taking time to understand their world.

How does our teaching remain relevant to the culture when most of what we teach is counter to the very culture in which we live? Herein lies the challenge! We must help our students see that the very issues confronting us today are not so different from those faced by some of the most inspiring and well-known biblical leaders. We have a tremendous opportunity to delve deeply into the characters' heart issues in the lessons we teach. God remains as present with us today as He was with the people we study and teach.

Helping Kids Relate

Making sure that kids recognize the relevance of the truths they're learning is just as important as assessing and assimilating what they're actually learning during your message time. Make sure your messages are directly relevant to kids' lives and offer them "take-home" tools to put to use right away. Exploring how sacrifices were made in Old Testament times is fascinating, but kids need to know ways we can give to God through our lives today. Always draw themes and messages back to kids' lives for the present and help kids discover how learning God's truths today impacts their faith tomorrow.

Excerpt from *Joy Builders* by Susan L. Lingo. Standard Publishing, 2001.

In my own experience teaching children in 5th and 6th grade, I have found that my students often think they already know every Bible lesson I prepare. I regularly see the look that says, *I dare you to teach me something I don't already know.* This is a perfect opportunity to begin training them to develop a biblical worldview. Challenge children to bring things to class that they have heard, read, and/or seen on television or in movies. Discuss these issues through the lens of biblical teaching. As you do this your students will begin to see the inconsistency of the world as it is measured against the timeless truth of God's Word. They will teach themselves as they dialogue, debate, and discuss issues in light of God's truth.

A child's worldview becomes a compass that will lead him through a very complex, contradictory, and confusing culture. It is the grid through which he will filter everything he encounters. George Barna, Directing Leader of the Barna Research Group, stresses the importance of instilling in children a well-established biblical worldview in his book *Transforming Children into Spiritual Champions: Why Children Should Be Your Church's #1 Priority* (Barna 2003).

Teaching with HEART requires understanding and remaining relevant to the culture confronting your students. Examine your own response to the culture, become familiar with the culture of your students, and work to develop a biblical worldview in the children you teach that will help them evaluate their own culture, as well as their response to it.

True to the Bible

The Word of God has the power to transforms lives and our teaching must remain true to the Bible in all aspects. Are we open to this transformation and are we helping the children we teach to be open themselves? One of the best ways to do this is to build familiarity with the God's Word. When children feel comfortable with the Bible and confident that they can read and understand what it says, they are better equipped to pattern their lives off of its truth.

One of the object lessons that I use in my teaching is to show the children my Bibles. First, I show them my tiny lace New Testament I was given when I was born. It is pretty but has never been used. Then I show them the Bible I received at my Lutheran confirmation in the eighth grade. It is white, has my name on the cover in gold, and looks almost exactly the same as when I received it over 40 years ago. These are my pretty Bibles.

Then I show them my Bibles from the last 25 years: my *NASB, NIV* and *NKJV*. They have worn covers, the pages are covered with

When children feel comfortable with the Bible they are better equipped to pattern their lives off of its truth.

notes, and they look tattered and torn. I ask them, "What is the difference between these Bibles?" The pretty Bibles were given to me as a child. In the church and school I attended as a child, we didn't use our Bibles. As a result mine remained pretty, white, and attractive. While they looked good, they were no good to me. My other Bibles may not look so good on the outside, but they have changed me on the inside. It is when we give ourselves to God's Word that we make ourselves available to its power to transform our lives.

We want our students to be comfortable with their Bibles. We want this comfort and familiarity with the Word of God to transform their lives in every aspect. Children must be taught how to remain true to the Bible in all areas of life—at home and at school, as well in church. Remaining true to the teachings found in the Bible begins with becoming familiar with what is found between its pages.

Becoming a Teacher with **HEART**

To become a teacher with HEART you must 1) lead and exemplify a holy life for your students, 2) maintain a teachable spirit, 3) remain age appropriate in the classroom, 4) strive to understand and teach to and through the culture of your students, and 5) remain true to the Word of God in all things. Let me challenge you to keep this foundation in mind as you study the techniques offered in this guide. Become a teacher with HEART for yourself and for the children you teach.

H.E.A.R.T.

Fill in the following chart to examine how you are currently teaching with HEART and what you desire to see in your students in these areas.

QUALITY	How is this evidenced in your life?	How would you like to see this evidenced in the lives of your students?
Holy Living		
Easy to Teach (a teachable spirit)		
Age Appropriate		
Relevant to Culture		
True to the Bible		

How to Become a Teacher with HEART

Use this review page to remember the key factors in becoming a teacher with HEART.

H _____ _____

- It is the call of Christ, combined with the power of the Holy Spirit, that cultivates a home in our hearts and lives for holiness.
- We will struggle to teach children how to foster holiness in their own lives if we are not making a concerted effort in our own.
- We must set an example for our students in speech, life, love, faith, and in purity.

E _____ to _____
(a teachable spirit)

- Remain approachable—teachable moments can pass you by. Live by God's to-do list.
- Be open to correction and remember that an apology can dissipate anger!
- Be willing to learn from others—even your students!
- Approach others with the same level of respect that you deesire. Children learn more from what you are than from what you say—model good manners.

A ____ _____

- Set up the learning environment so that it's appropriate to the age of the students you teach.
- Strive to make your classroom learner-centered while remaining in charge as the teacher—this is a delicate balance.
- Communicate using age-appropriate words that your students can hear and understand—speak their language!
- Use bridge-building words and avoid critical and condescending words that become roadblocks to communication.

R _____
to the _____

- Get to know the culture your students live in—take time to understand their culture and make your teaching relevant by building relationships.
- Use tools of your students' culture (such as media) to engage them in the lesson.
- Help your students develop a biblical worldview to help them process the issues they are confronted with on a daily basis.
- Make sure that your own worldview is biblically grounded before you begin to help your students understand their culture.

T _____ to the _____

- Help children build familiarity with the Word of God—when children feel comfortable with the Bible and confident that they can read and understand what it says, they are better equipped to pattern their lives off of its truth.
- As a teacher become familiar with God's Word and open your life to your students to help them see how God's Word has impacted you (through showing them your own study tools, etc.).

Chapter 3

Cherishing and Challenging Children to Fit God's Design of Their Personalities

A Teacher with HEART understands that God formed and knows every part of the children she teaches.

Scripture: "Before I formed you in the womb I knew you" (Jeremiah 1:5).

Teaching Objective: To understand and embrace the personalities God has given the children we teach so that we may love them more effectively.

I believe that God imprints each of us with a pattern specially designed for His purpose. One of these patterns can be identified as our personalities. In this chapter I will refer to four personalities that are identified in the DISC model (Voges). I believe that we each have a strong, dominant personality and a weaker, secondary one, as well as parts of all four. I also believe that when we are reborn into God's family, we become a more balanced blend of the four personalities as part of the sanctification process.

We do not study personality types so we can say, "Well, that's just the way I am. I'll never change. That's the way God made me." Rather we give our personality strengths back to God to be used for His service. Likewise, we come to Him on our knees with our weaknesses. In our weakness He is able to make us strong. By His grace we can overcome, and He can work through our weaknesses. Thus, through the special personality God gave each of us, we can bring honor and glory back to God.

We must remember, however, that we all tend to see life through the grid of our individual personalities. We often assume that we are right because this is how God made us. Hence, everyone else should function this way as well. At the core of this is the sin of pride. Deep down, we all think we know it all. Jesus teaches us to live for others and to give up our need for pride, ownership, and control. As we affirm the individuality of others and help our students to enjoy diversity and learn from one other, we begin to understand Christ's love for each of us.

In order to illustrate how the four basic personalities fall within certain guidelines of behavior, I will use the model on the following page.

The DISC model is one of several models of personality development. In addition, John Trent and Gary Smalley have written a delightful book to help children understand their personality differences called *The Treasure Tree,* which is also identified in the following chart (1992).

It is interesting to note that of the numerous personality development models used, all include four patterns that are all consistent with one another. The name or label of each personality, however, is not as important as what we do with what God has given each of us.

> We all tend to see life through the grid of our individual personalities.

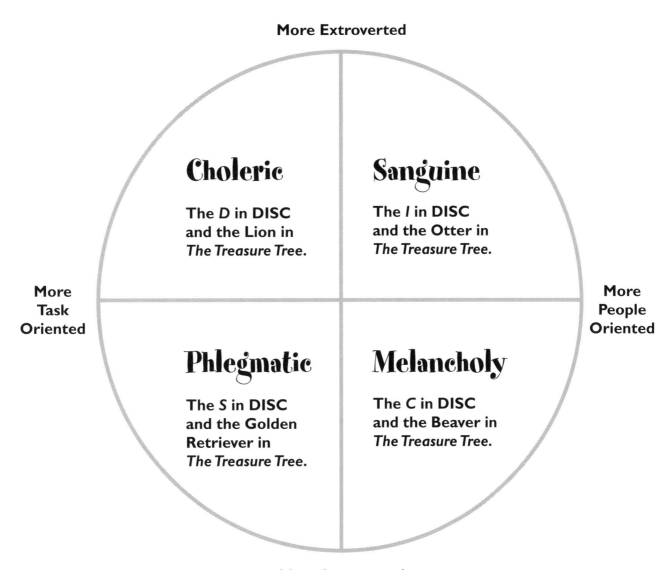

More Extroverted

Choleric

The *D* in **DISC**
and the Lion in
The Treasure Tree.

Sanguine

The *I* in **DISC**
and the Otter in
The Treasure Tree.

**More
Task
Oriented**

**More
People
Oriented**

Phlegmatic

The *S* in **DISC**
and the Golden
Retriever in
The Treasure Tree.

Melancholy

The *C* in **DISC**
and the Beaver in
The Treasure Tree.

More Introverted

The goal of studying personalities is to understand, reach, and teach children more effectively.

In this chapter we will look at each of these four personalities identified in the DISC model and identify them as children we commonly see in our classrooms. I will provide you with practical information on how you can cherish and challenge children and their personalities more effectively. Each of us has components of our personality/temperament that fall into each of the four quadrants. For purposes of discussion, however, we will identify the strongest from the four and focus on the strengths and weaknesses of each individual personality. The goal in all of this is to understand, reach, and teach children more effectively.

Understanding Choleric Children (*D* in the DISC Model)

Choleric children want CONTROL at any cost! It is incredulous to them that someone else is in charge. They assume they should be; therefore, teachers of these children are locked in a battle of wills from the very beginning. Dr. James Dobson has called this the strong-willed child (*The New Strong Willed Child,* 2004). The secret of handling these children is to use the words, "You're in charge of . . ." It's amazing how well this works. Let them be in charge of things you want them to be in charge of like cleaning up their area, completing their work, remembering to bring their Bibles, and organizing their workspace. Give them tasks to be in charge of, or they will simply try to take over on their own.

These children, when properly cherished and challenged, often grow up to be great leaders, pastors, and presidents of companies. They have the gifts to do great things for the Lord. The challenge lies in channeling their drive to direct and teaching them obedience. When they feel they have control over at least some aspects of their lives, they are able to exhibit a more submissive spirit to the authority figures in their lives.

Choleric Children in the Classroom

Characteristics:

In your classroom, the choleric children are those who

- are energetic
- are strong-willed
- exhibit natural leadership
- want to be in charge
- can be bossy or domineering

How to Spot Them:

Choleric children will enter the room with A-T-T-I-T-U-D-E! They come in with an agenda and have a presence about them that commands attention. They are activity driven and may push to accomplish things. They are definite DOERS.

These choleric students are sizing you up as the teacher. If they sense a void in your authority or a lack of leadership, they will attempt to move in and take over. If there is a new teacher who seems unsure of herself, or a substitute teacher who does not know the routine, these children will attempt to commandeer the classroom. On one hand they have been gifted with natural leadership capabilities. However, on the other hand they can often be very bossy and domineering.

Cholerics seem to radiate power and have usually already gained a following. Other children seem naturally drawn to them, whether or not they are making good choices. The other students seem to sense that they are in the presence of a leader and follow suit.

Choleric children want control at any cost and they will start with you!

What's a Teacher to Do?

As a teacher, it is wise to make friends with these children. One way to do this is to talk with them in private and say, "I can see that God has given you great leadership gifts. I would like to put you in charge of some things in our classroom. You can be a great help to me." Cholerics have a strong need to be in charge, so when you speak their language, they hear *in charge* and respond well. They can either be a great help to you or a continual hindrance. That ball is in your court! Don't fear these children, God has put them in your class to help you!

Choleric Curtis

Choleric Curtis enters the classroom, looking it over as another challenge to conquer. The look in his eyes, his body language, and the tone of his voice all seem to say *I'm here. I dare you to teach me something I don't already know.* He wants control at any cost, and he will start with you. He is a driving, demanding, decisive person who likes to do and to be in charge. He has a natural presence that seems to lend itself to leadership.

We have all experienced a Choleric Curtis in our classrooms. He is your basic control freak. He is the child who will give you your gray hairs! But he also can be the most fulfilling child to teach. Don't be afraid of his energy and desire to dominate. See these as potential leadership gifts. God has called you, oh dear teacher with HEART, to lovingly channel his energy to be used for the Kingdom. Take time to get to know him. He will respond to your love and will be a great helper in leading your class. Because of his gifts he will be in charge of something in his lifetime. Let's just make sure it's in God's Kingdom.

How to Cherish:

Do . . .

- Take time to get to know him.
- Show him you acknowledge and appreciate his leadership gifts.
- Love and appreciate him.

Don't . . .

- Criticize him in front of his peers.
- Bribe him to be good.
- Try to match him will for will!

How to Challenge:

Do . . .

- Give him things to be in charge of that are within perimeters that you set and that contribute to your classroom goals.
- Allow him to be a positive leader in your classroom.
- Give him choices that are permissible.

Don't . . .

- Put him down in front of his peers; he will lose trust in you and it will be a difficult relationship to repair.
- Give him rules that may seem legalistic— guidelines work better for him.
- Say, "You will do as I say!"

Sanguine children may compromise what they believe to receive approval.

Understanding Sanguine Children (*I* in the DISC Model)

These children are sunshine. They simply want to have fun and to love and be loved. They tell you how wonderful you are. They hug you and bring you presents. They are, however, forgetful, talkative, and impulsive. They have never met a stranger and are at home in any group. They love people and interacting with them. They want approval at any cost. They may compromise on what they believe just to get approval from someone they admire. With these children you have to help them develop strength of character.

The sanguine child's criteria for measuring the validity of an experience are usually by the degree of fun it provided. The following is a typical kind of conversation a parent might have with a sanguine child after church:

"How was Sunday school today?"

"Great—we had so much fun!"

"What was the lesson about?"

"Huh? Ah. I think I forgot."

"Did you remember your Bible?"

"Hm . . . no, I think I forgot it."

"Do you remember where?"

"Um . . . I think it was in the bathroom when I was talking to Jenny. Mom, we have this great thing planned for next Friday night. It will be so much fun! I'm going to wear my . . ."

"Honey, did you get permission to go?"

"Um . . . I forgot. Sorry, Mom. But Mom, please, can I go? It will be so fun!"

When properly cherished and challenged, these children can easily realize their God-given potential. They can often rise to the top on their own as well, since they have a strong, natural sense of who they are. *To know me is to love me* is often their motto, and they say it with a twinkle in their eye. They enjoy being who they are and feel certain everyone else will too if they just take time to know them.

Sanguine Children in the Classroom:

Characteristics:

In your classroom, the sanguine children are those who

- are extroverted—outgoing!
- have fun
- are happy
- seem talkative
- appear playful

How to Spot Them:

This is the child who rushes in to give you a big hug and then checks out the social scene. She is a joy to have in class but may forget to not talk to her friend while you are teaching, as well as to bring her Bible or hold on to her papers.

Sanguines usually have a group of children around them and they are having a good time. They are happy and attract others with their fun and upbeat personalities. Their main goal in class is to get caught up on what has been happening with each other. I have had to say to them, "May I interrupt your party so that I may impart a few life changing truths?" They are easy to get along with, quick to apologize, and often respond, "I'm sorry . . . sure!" But after a few minutes, they continue on with their social lives.

They are the cheerleaders in the class who encourage others along the way. They smile easily, find a fun way to solve difficult issues, love others easily, and are easily loved in return.

What's a Teacher to Do?

Their key word is fun, so when you want to motivate them in the classroom, you have to clothe it with the word fun. "Let's get through this lesson and then I have a game for us to play that will help us remember the key concepts. You will love it, it's so much fun!" For these children, if something is fun, it is valid. If it isn't fun, it isn't worth doing. They are fun students to have in the classroom, but you will have to tone down their fun at times.

Sanguine Siena

Sanguine Siena enters the classroom willing and eager to meet her new friends. Every one is a potential best friend, and she has never met a stranger. She has a twinkle in her eye and a jump to her step. Everything has the potential to be fun when Siena is involved. In fact, all you have to do is say "This will really be fun!" and she will be the president of your fan club. She brings joy, love, and laughter wherever she goes.

How to Cherish:

Do . . .

- Be positive!
- Tell her you love her just as she is!
- Remember she responds better to fun and games. Yes, you can include some in your teaching and still get the job done!

Don't . . .

- Allow her to manipulate you or others with her natural charm.
- Let her get away with things just because she's cute and fun.
- Allow her to get off the hook by apologizing without accepting responsibility.

How to Challenge:

Do . . .

- Help her to overcome her forgetfulness.
- Lovingly remind her to turn off her talking switch.
- Use her natural gifts of fun and humor to challenge her to do better—she has a high desire to please and will respond well to this.

Don't . . .

- Come on too strong with your plan to make her better or she will fold.
- Be critical in a cold way, she will wilt before your very eyes.
- Rain on her parade because she is the eternal optimist.

Understanding Phlegmatic Children (*S in the DISC Model*)

These children are a joy because they are so easygoing. They make parents and teachers look good because they rarely act up. They are quiet, easy to please, pleasant to get along with, and patient. However, they can also be stubborn, sneaky or lazy. Properly guided, they can become some of the best servants in God's kingdom because they are the peacemakers. They don't get bent out of shape over many of the things that children with the other three personalities do.

When properly approached and guided, these children are amazing leaders. They have excellent internal organization. They can keep it together while others are losing it around them.

I always love having phlegmatic children in my classroom. Long ago, in the old millennium, ladies often put shoulder pads made of foam rubber under sweaters and jackets. One day I was putting something up on the board and was working quickly when I heard this lovely ripple of laughter. Since I had learned who was usually the cause of these by now, I looked at my phlegmatic student, who, of course, looked so very innocent. I asked, "What did you say, sweet darling?" He replied, "Well, Mrs. Capehart, I said your bra fell off." Of course, the class was laughing hysterically. I tried to remain calm as I replied, "Darlin', I appreciate you sharing that, but if it really happened, I think I would be the first to know." To which, he replied with a perfectly straight face, "It really did, Mrs. Capehart, please look . . ." I whirled around and there on the floor was my foam shoulder pad, which perhaps to the untrained eye could look like a bra! Yikes! Now, you probably will never forget who these precious phlegmatic children are!

Phlegmatic Children in the Classroom

Characteristics:

In your classroom, the phlegmatic children are those who
- appear reserved
- are people-oriented
- act as the peacemakers
- are compliant and pleasant
- can be sneaky and stubborn

How To Spot Them:

Phlegmatic children come into the classroom and quietly look around with a soft smile on their faces. They slowly check out the scene before they get involved. They are happy to enjoy things while remaining on the periphery. However, they are not on the

outside because the other students reject them; in fact, they are quietly popular with everyone.

They are natural peacemakers. They do not offend any of the other personality types. The choleric students like them because they have no power agenda. The sanguine children like them because they have a great sense of humor, albeit, a quiet wit, and they do not compete with the silly sanguines. The melancholy children like them because they are gentle and kind and feel a common desire for peace. Thus, they are often on the periphery by choice, they like observing and enjoying things vicariously.

What's a Teacher to Do?

Phlegmatic children in the classroom make teaching a joy for everyone. They are the most easygoing of the personality types. They actually obey you and are cooperative with whatever you have planned. In fact, teachers have been known to pray to have more of these children in their classrooms!

However, while they are sweet and steady, they have a sinful nature as well, and may be stubborn and/or sneaky at times. You will see their stubborn side when you try to hurry them. They don't do fast and will show you their passive-aggressive side which can be very stubborn. Their sneaky side is harder to find because they disguise it so well with their sweet side. So I pray that when they do something wrong, they will get caught!

Phlegmatic children only do the little mischievous things, and always behind your back. They don't do the big in-your-face kind of things like a choleric child would do. They like to make little jokes, get everyone else going, and then when you turn and look, these are the children who will appear so sweet and innocent. It may take awhile before you figure out that it is these children who are creating these mysterious ripples of laughter. They are easy to bring back into compliance, however, and you will enjoy their dry wit.

Because these are the easy students, they may begin to see themselves as the good kids. Since they rarely get in trouble, they may think they are above the system. Also, don't allow them to get lazy because they will often take the easy route.

> **Phlegmatics make teachers look good because they are quiet, easy to please, pleasant, and patient.**

Phlegmatic Patrick

Phlegmatic Patrick is your peacemaker. You will love having him in your classroom. He won't demand your time and attention, and thus you must be careful to not forget him. His personality is so easy to teach and discipline, but he is a sinner like everyone else and has his weaknesses. Remember, he can be stubborn or lazy, especially when pushed. Keep in mind, also, that he is sneaky and may do little things behind your back, although you may never suspect him because he looks so sweet. He can get the rest of the class going and looks innocent as you try and figure out who started the party. I do encourage you to pray that when he does something wrong, he will get caught or he may become desensitized to the issues of sin.

How to Cherish:

Do . . .

- Understand that he is often content to be alone—gently approach him (he pulls back from forceful people).
- Quietly let him know you care.
- Enjoy his quiet wit.

Don't . . .

- Assume his desire to be alone is problem related.
- Pair him up with a loud, rowdy child and expect him to manage the difficult child.
- Put him on center stage.

How to Challenge:

Do . . .

- Allow him his space to grow.
- Recognize his amazing internal organizational gifts.
- Remember that he is a sinner like everyone else, and realize that he may be mischievous when you aren't looking.

Don't . . .

- Push or hurry him, you will see his stubborn side.
- Let his easygoing nature cause him to become lazy.
- Let him get away with things because he looks sweet and innocent.

> Don't tell melancholy children to "Lighten up!" Reflect their feelings and encourage them.

Understanding Melancholy Children (*C* in the DISC Model)

These children are determined to do it right. They are born perfectionists. If a first attempt isn't perfect, they may give up in total discouragement. They are often serious, genius prone, artistic, moody, and deep thinkers. Childhood is not their happiest hour. They will be happier as adults. Play doesn't mean as much to them as to the sanguine child.

Melancholy children may need help to lighten up and become more positive. You can help them accept themselves and the world as it is. Love them unconditionally. While these children do not seek attention, they respond deeply to your loving, encouraging words, especially when you say them in private. I enjoy talking with these children privately. I often say something like, "Childhood (or teen years) may not be your favorite season of life. Sometimes you may feel like you don't enjoy life like it seems the others do. But I can see that God is doing great things inside of you, and I believe the best is yet to come. Hang in there." This encourages them because they often hear people say, "Lighten up, these are the best years of your life!" Inwardly, they may think, *If this is the best life has, I am not sure I want the rest!*

Great things may come from these children, but it is usually with a great deal of internal struggle and pain. This child is like a grown-up in a little body. They see the ideal and perfection in their mind, but because we live in a fallen and sinful world, everyone and everything falls short. Therefore, they can become easily depressed. They have great sensitivity and will be truly content, productive adults who will accomplish great things for the kingdom.

Melancholy Children in the Classroom

Characteristics:

In your classroom, the melancholy children are those who

- are quiet and often reserved
- can be introverted and easily overwhelmed by their surroundings
- might seem overly sensitive
- are very conscientious and sometimes perfectionists

How to Spot Them:

These are not the students who will rush in to hug and talk to you. These children enter the classroom quietly and often self-consciously. They often have a serious look on their faces and may appear to be cautious. They are very conscientious, compliant, and careful. They want to do what is right but are very cautious for fear of making a mistake. They like the routine to be predictable and don't respond well to change. They often look overwhelmed or overstimulated, do not readily jump in, and are reserved.

They lack the outward appearance of self-confidence that the choleric and sanguine children have, and for sure, are not easygoing like the phlegmatic children are.

What's a Teacher to Do?

Don't say "Lighten up," because they can't. Simply reflect the feeling and find words to encourage them. Rather than being a cheerleader to get these children to be more positive, you can be more effective in helping them get unstuck from their melancholy "paralysis of analysis" by reflecting their feelings.
For example:

The teacher asks the class, "What did you learn from the chapel lesson today?"

Melancholy child: "I didn't like it. I don't want to go back." Teacher: "Oh come on, it was a wonderful lesson. I just loved it. Surely you can find something positive to say about chapel, can't you?"

Your melancholy student responds with a resounding "No!" or a whimpering whine, and it escalates from there.
Try this approach instead:

"I can see you are not happy about something that happened in chapel."

When you reflect the feeling rather than the facts, you can get farther with these children. If they feel heard, they can begin to move their focus from the negative to the positive. Their unhappiness is usually over something small and once the feeling is reflected, they can begin to move forward.

A word to the wise: use this technique sparingly to see if it is going to be effective. If the child continues to whine, simply say, "I am sorry you feel that way. When you are ready to talk without whining or complaining, I will be happy to talk with you." The bottom line is that some sensitive children just need to be heard and then can turn their attitudes around. Some children are whiners and we don't want to reinforce that in our students.

Melancholy Mei Li

Melancholy Mei Li is the child who usually sees the glass half empty instead of half full. She requires a great deal of encouragement. When asked about something, she will often focus on the negative rather than the positive.

If you are upset, she is sure it's her fault. If you have a discipline scene with a choleric child, Melancholy Mei Li is the one who may look afraid. You need to go to her quietly and privately and whisper, "I am not upset with you, and you are doing great. Thank you."

She often doubts herself and takes everything personally. She is not the one to misbehave and is your rule follower, however, she often feels guilty for no reason. So when someone else breaks a rule, she is the first to notice, and often, the first to report it. Somehow, it helps alleviate her inward, self-imposed guilt. Thank her for wanting to help, but lovingly tell her that you will take care of things. You don't want to create a tattle-tail! She is a very serious, deep thinking child and a blessing to have in the classroom.

How to Cherish:

Do . . .

- Encourage! Encourage! Encourage! Make sure you tell her in some way every day how well she is doing—her little bucket has lots of holes in it!
- Reflect her feelings.
- Realize she feels self-anointed be the one to point out what everyone else is doing wrong because deep down she is terrified of being wrong herself.

Don't . . .

- Allow her to whine or constantly complain.
- Allow her to be critical of everyone and everything.
- Allow her to succumb to her own pity party.

How to Challenge:

Do . . .

- Encourage! Encourage! Encourage! She needs encouragement and will take to it like a duck to water.
- Understand that she gets "paralysis of analysis" and the "melancholy freeze"! Again, the only way to get her going is to encourage her.
- Remember that childhood may not be her finest hour. She will be a very content adult, you just have to help her get through this season called childhood. Please don't say, "These are the best years of your life," but instead, "The best is yet to come."

Don't . . .

- Point out her faults as constructive criticism.
- Give her too much to do—her perfectionist qualities slow her down.
- Say "I know you can do better, why didn't you?" Whoops, crash landing!

Facing the Day of Reckoning

Parents love their children, which is what we want from them. But in that love is often some blindness to recognizing their children's faults. Parents also want you to love their children and see only the best. Therefore, when you have an issue and need to talk to parents, it may be hard for them to hear the words. Remember, fear is often at the core. They are afraid that you may think they are bad parents. Therefore, be aware of coming on too strong, so that the parent doesn't become defensive. That is not a healthy way to build relationships with parents.

Try this formula to build a positive partnership with parents.

First, always speak with them in private so you don't embarrass them in front of others. Find something positive to say about their child first: "I like the way Johnny has such great, creative ideas!"

Next, understate the negative and clothe it with an I statement: "I am having a little problem with Johnny wanting to share his ideas in class without raising his hand. I wonder if you could help me think of a way I can help him to remember to wait to share his ideas." This puts the parents in a positive position to help you and thus, empowers them.

Finally, close the discussion with a prayer and a positive, proactive plan to help Johnny.

Identifying Personalities in Your Students

As you think about your classroom and the children you teach, answer the following questions to help you identify each of the four personalities in your students.

1. Am I responding appropriately to the personalities I teach?

2. Can I see myself in these personality patterns? What personality do I think I most strongly exhibit?

3. In what ways are my students different from me?

4. How do I embrace these differences?

5. Have I identified with my students via our similarities? Through our differences?

6. What unique personality pattern do I see in each of my students?

7. What am I doing to cherish their uniqueness?

8. What am I doing to challenge each student to be the best she can be?

9. Am I praying for each student in terms of God's purpose for her unique personality?

Cherishing and Challenging Each Personality

Fill in the chart below to explore ways that you can cherish and challenge your students based on their unique personalities.

Choleric

I can cherish this student by:
-
-
-

I can effectively challenge this student by:
-
-
-

Sanguine

I can cherish this student by:
-
-
-

I can effectively challenge this student by:
-
-
-

My Personality

Phlegmatic

I can cherish this student by:
-
-
-

I can effectively challenge this student by:
-
-
-

Melancholy

I can cherish this student by:
-
-
-

I can effectively challenge this student by:
-
-
-

Cherishing and Challenging Children to Fit God's Design of Their Learning Modalities

A Teacher with HEART understands that teaching God's Word is the most important thing but that each child learns differently.

Scripture: "These commandments that I give you today are to be upon your hearts. Impress them on your children. Talk about them when you sit at home and when you walk along the road, when you lie down and when you get up. Tie them as symbols on your hands and bind them on your foreheads. Write them on the doorframes of your houses and on your gates" (Deuteronomy 6:6-9).

Teaching Objective: To understand and embrace the God-given learning modalities of children so that we can teach them more effectively.

> **Young children are learning at an incredibly rapid rate, never again to be repeated.**

Understanding Learning Modalities

Observe a young child for a few minutes and watch how he takes in information. He makes a grab for an item and immediately takes it to his mouth. As he gets older, he smells it instead of putting it in his mouth. He sees it, touches it, and then shakes it to see if it makes a sound. He combines all of his five senses to truly get an understanding of what this object is all about. In this experience he begins the lifelong process of organizing and classifying the information he encounters via his five senses.

Learning modalities are the processes through which children learn. A modality is a sensory unit that enables us to take in information. All children are multisensory learners. They learn best when they can see something, hear it, touch it, and with little ones, taste it and sometimes smell it.

The four main modalities for school-age children are:

1. Visual modality: see it
2. Auditory modality: hear it
3. Tactile modality: touch it
4. Kinesthetic modality: do it

Children learn through their senses on their own during the preschool years. To assist the learning process, here is an easy three-step plan that achieves good results when used:

1. Isolate what the child is to learn.
2. Classify each step of the process.
3. Refine the learning process.

For example, let's say you want to teach a child about colors. First, isolate exactly what it is you want to teach. Lay out three colors. (I use tablets of colored papers or paint chips.) Then classify the colors. "This is red. This is yellow. This is blue." Then ask the child, "Show me red. Show me yellow. Show me blue." Next, ask the child to name the colors for you. If he can, then you can continue on to step #3. If not, go back to the beginning and name the colors. After an extensive time of teaching all of the main colors, you can continue to the third step in which you refine what was learned in the first two steps. You could, for example, have the child make a color wheel and shade the colors from dark to light.

This three-step process occurs naturally and spontaneously within children. That is the very reason that children appear to be geniuses. Indeed, they are! If adults had to assimilate the vast volumes of information that a young child does, we would collapse from exhaustion. Young children are learning at an incredibly rapid rate, never again to be repeated. They are constantly taking in data via multisensory modalities, organizing, and assimilating it. So why do problems occur when the child enters a classroom?

How Teachers Teach

Teachers often do not teach in the way that children learn best—either because they don't know how to or because they teach based on their own learning modalities. Most teachers are visual learners and so they teach visually. Therefore, classrooms continue to be havens for visual learners. These are the children who learn best by seeing something. They are usually good readers, can quickly grasp things that they see, and enjoy worksheets, workbooks, and similar things that many teachers use.

Church and school curriculum packets often come with visual aids, and therefore it is easier to remember to incorporate the visual items. There are many Bible story videos that children like to see, as well as interactive video activities. The visual sense is the one most easily incorporated into teaching. This is perfect for children who are visual learners (approximately one-third of all children), but what about children who are not visual learners?

A smaller percentage (about 30%) of children are auditory learners, which means that they need to hear the information and talk about it in order to best assimilate it. Talking usually occurs in the teaching process, and these children can then grasp the subject at that time. But when they go back to their places for seatwork, suddenly it is all "Greek" to them. It is vital for a teacher to explain the subject matter to them again and allow them to verbalize what they are learning.

As the teacher is presenting the lesson, it is wise to include times for verbal interactions with the students. For example, if the teacher is presenting a lesson about David, the students may tune the teacher out thinking they already know this lesson. Taking time to ask questions to check the students' understanding and involve them in using critical thinking skills takes them to deeper level of learning. For example, in the lesson about David, a teacher could ask, "How do you think David felt when he saw Goliath? Have you ever been really afraid of something or someone and the problem or the person seemed to grow before your very eyes? What happened when you prayed about it? What did God do to help you?" Remember, auditory learners retain 50 percent of what they have heard, and in order for them to complete the learning loop, they must talk about it. Hearing brings in the information to the halfway point, and talking about it brings it to 100 percent

Teachers often teach based on their own learning modalities.

for retention. So to remember it, retain it, and retrieve it, students MUST talk about it.

But wait a minute. Almost one half of all children need to touch something or do it to understand it. These children often can cruise through a preschool or kindergarten program because the teachers use many things that children can touch and do. But when first grade hits, suddenly these children have a problem. Why? Because they cannot learn as well with just visual or auditory input. They have to touch, and there is often nothing to touch except a book, pencil, or worksheet, and those don't count as tactile learning tools! Take a visit to your local Christian bookstore—they often have a children's section full of wonderful, hands-on manipulatives.

If you are teaching Sunday school, make a list of your lesson topics. Purchase some clear plastic bins (when they are on sale) and use a permanent marker to write the lesson topics on the outside of the clear bins. Stack the bins in a storage closet or corner of your classroom or garage. In time you will see how quickly these get filled up. You will soon notice these bins filled with leftover toys from your own children, household items, and garage sale items and before you know it, you have manipulatives for each lesson!

Take a lesson about Noah, for example. There are Noah's ark items everywhere. I used my children's old toys, found a baby toy hammer, little animals at the dollar store, and a toy ark at a garage sale. Also, if you let the parents know your lesson topics, they will happily donate things. Try it—you will be surprised at how quickly your bins fill up!

Identifying and teaching using the various learning modalities can remove frustration and discipline challenges from the class-room. When a student is engaged in his learning style comfort zone, he feels at home. He is relaxed, actively engaged, and is using his energy to learn.

Children have an innate desire to want to learn. The reason they appear to tune out the learning process is because it has been presented in a way that is boring to them and not in their learning style comfort zone. Imagine if you went to another country and couldn't understand or speak the language. You couldn't connect, communicate, or feel a part of things. You might appear to be de-tached from things, when in reality, there weren't avenues for you to attach to the environment. So it is with learning. When we speak the learning language of a student, she hears us and connects. It also communicates consideration to each child.

Children tune out because information is not presented to them in their learning style comfort zone.

Visual Learners

Visual children are always on the look out! They notice when you have put something new up on the wall or added a new learning activity on a shelf or in a learning center. They pay attention to the visual world and feel empowered when they are encouraged to see if they can find something new such as an item added on the Bible timeline. Play the Detective Game or I Spy with these children: "I spy something new in our classroom to do today, who can see what it is and where it is?"

Characteristics:

Visual learners

- Need to see something to understand it
- Often roll their eyes up and to the right or left as they are being talked to because they are trying to picture it in their mind
- Like to write things down
- Often need quiet in order to concentrate
- Can handle a lot of visual input like charts, graphs, pictures, etc., but usually like it orderly for maximum concentration
- Generally learn to read easily

How to Spot Them:

Visual Victoria is often looking around. She notices new things that she can see. "Teacher, did you get a haircut? It looks nice." "Teacher, I like the new bulletin board." She loves visuals and will pay great attention to anything she can see, especially if it is new.

How to Cherish:

- She watches body language. She observes you closely and sees the look in your eyes. You can communicate with her easily with a smile and through your eyes. A smile speaks volumes to her. Likewise, a frown can shut her down for quite awhile.
- A sticker on a paper, a written word of encouragement, and a happy face on a paper can encourage her greatly. If you send a note card during the week, she child will save it and reread it many times.
- A chart where she can apply smiley stickers, or check things off to mark progress will help her keep up with what you're teaching in class.

How to Challenge:

- Try using an improvement chart in her notebook or Bible where she can collect stars or stickers marking improvements. If she is truly doing well, you can post it on the bulletin board. If you are working on a behavior and the signs of improvement are not steady, it may be better not to post it publicly. Visual Victoria is very responsive to what others see and if the progress isn't positive, she may shut down. If she is embarrassed, she might just give up and not try at all.
- A sticky note or a note card that says, "I know you can do better. Let's go for the gold!" will encourage her heart and boost her confidence.
- Speak her learning language: "I *see* you trying harder. I know you can do it. I can't wait to *see* what you will do next week!"

Auditory Learners

For auditory learners the key to learning is to minimize visual distractions. Let them talk. Even let them tape-record things and listen to them.

One moment of waiting to speak can seem like an hour to them. Lovingly acknowledge their need, "I know you want to talk and I am going to call on you. Show me how quietly you can wait."

Characteristics:

Auditory learners

- Learn 50 percent by what they hear and 50 percent by what they talk about—they must talk in order to remember, retrieve, and retain what they learn
- Like lots of auditory input
- Like to tell you things in complete detail
- Love to talk and often have to tell you their entire day in sequence

How to Spot Them:

Auditory Ashley loves to talk. In fact, at age 4, she talks whether anyone is in the room or not. When she gets older she will learn to raise her hand but at the same time will shout, "I raised my hand! I raised my hand!" After she has learned to raise her hand and wait to be called upon, she will look like she could hyperventilate and pass out if you don't call on her!

How to Cherish:

- Tell her how much you care—remember people don't care how much you know until they know how much you care.
- She hears your tone of voice. If she can hear your displeasure she may shut down.
- Sing the rules to her—even older students like to hear music, rhymes or raps.

How to Challenge:

- Use verbal challenges, "I know this is hard, but I believe you can do it."
- Encourage her effort so she will keep on wanting to try. "I like the way you tried so hard to complete this project. Keep trying, I know you can do it!"
- Apply scriptural truths: "How do you think Jesus would handle this situation? What do you think Jesus would do? What does the Bible say about this? Can you show me how you could 'do to others' (Matthew 7:12)?"

Tactile Learners

Sometimes teachers think if a child is fiddling with something in his hands he isn't paying attention. For a tactile child, this is exactly what he needs in order to learn. These children use the clicker on a pen over and over or take two pencils and create a percussion section. Put something constructive in their hands that will facilitate learning and not be a distraction. For example, I sometimes let older students doodle as I read to them, as long as it is related to the lesson. I may allow younger children to have modeling clay at their place and create things related to the lesson as I read. The key is that it remains related to the lesson.

Characteristics:

Tactile learners

- Like to touch things
- Have hands that are always busy
- Prefer hands-on learning
- Like manipulatives
- Can be taught adaptive tactile skills, like highlighting and taking notes

How to Spot Them:

Tactile Ty is a learner whose hands are always busy. He lives to doodle, make paper airplanes, or mess with the person next to him.

I have worked with many tactile learners in my years of teaching. One very vivid memory I have is of a particular tactile learner who always liked to touch what I was wearing. One day he kept touching my dress and finally said, "Your dress is like the curtains in our kitchen." This was either a very keen tactile observation or an insult.

How to Cherish:

- Provide things for him to touch that are productive and related to what you are teaching.
- Provide manipulatives to facilitate learning.
- Provide tactile tools that can enhance his learning—but make it clear, "This is a privilege. If you abuse it, you lose it."

How to Challenge:

- Offer him hands-on learning materials.
- Give him things to fix, take apart, and put back together.
- Teach him tactile adaptive skills, such as note taking, highlighting, and making note cards, and let him create his own tactile learning system.

Kinesthetic Kenan

Kinesthetic Learners

This is probably the most ignored and least understood of the learning modalities. That is because much of the adult world runs on visual or auditory tracks. However, technology has dramatically changed this over the past decade. Thanks to computers, e-mails, and all of the techie toys, there are more things for kinesthetic learners to do and to touch. As adults we learn to adjust to the system and therefore forget the importance of interactive learning. We think of it as just a part of childhood. However, for kinesthetic learners this is the best format for learning.

Children who live with attention deficit disorder (ADD) or attention deficit hyperactivity disorder (ADHD) need kinesthetic learning opportunities and often calm down when they are able to touch things

Characteristics:

Kinesthetic learners

- Need to move in order to learn
- May seem hyperactive and are often labeled as such because they are restless and frustrated when they don't have something to touch
- Learn best by doing and interacting with an item
- May need to minimize their visual and auditory input and work alone with a hands-on item

How to Spot Them:

You can always spot little Kinesthetic Kenan. He is always on the move. (Please note: most preschool children are kinesthetic. This does not mean that they are kinesthetic learners. It means that they are developmentally in a kinesthetic stage.) Die-hard kinesthetic learners must do in order to learn. If we understand how God made Kinesthetic Kenan's body, we can see his constant movement as a gift to be harnessed into growing God's kingdom rather than as a disruption.

How to Cherish:
- Allow active learning.
- Provide positive opportunities for him to move and do.
- Channel his energy into constructive activities.

How to Challenge:
- Affirm his high energy level and challenge him to use it in positive ways.
- Give him constructive outlets, such as setting up chairs, doing errands, athletics, and being in charge—this helps harness his energy.
- Teach him techniques such as reading while riding a stationary bike, completing tasks and then taking a break, and strategies for self-management.

When you look at this child, ask yourself, "What can all this energy do if properly channeled into building God's kingdom?" Whew! The Lord will begin to give you His picture of what He wants from this child. We tend to see all the energy of a kinesthetic learner as a discipline issue, and indeed it can be if not dealt with properly. Instead, however, let's view this energy as a gift and find ways to harness it for God's kingdom. This certainly is true for children affected by ADD/ADHD. They are abundantly gifted, we just have to look beyond some of their seemingly bothersome characteristics.

ADD and ADHD: What It Is and Is Not

Children who test high as being tactile or kinesthetic learners are often mislabeled as having ADD (Attention Deficit Disorder) or ADHD (Attention Deficit Hyperactivity Disorder). While there are many common characteristics between these learning styles and these disorders, we cannot assume that ADD or ADHD affects every tactile or kinesthetic learner.

Children who are affected by ADD often test as tactile learners. Children with ADHD test as kinesthetic learners. However, as I mentioned before, not every child who is a tactile or kinesthetic learner is affected by ADD or ADHD. I have previously written two books on the topics of ADD and ADHD and feel strongly the need for teachers to understand what it is and what it is not.

What it is not:

Let's first look at what it is not. It is not simply a personality or learning style. For example, let's look at each personality (see Chapter 3) and see what characteristics might appear to be ADD (without the hyperactivity component) or ADHD (with the hyperactive/acting out component).

Choleric Curtis: His need for control and intense energy may be perceived as ADHD.

Sanguine Siena: Her sometimes spaceyness, silliness, and forgetfulness may be perceived as ADD or ADHD.

Phlegmatic Patrick: His quiet nature may be perceived as ADD.

Melancholy Mei Li: Her emotional meltdowns may be perceived as ADD.

It is obviously easy to misunderstand and, therefore, misdiagnose certain personality and learning characteristics as ADD or ADHD. Research also shows us that there are at least six different forms of

It is easy to misunderstand and misdiagnose ADD and ADHD.

ADD and ADHD. If we take all of the different variables of personality and learning characteristics, factor in six different kinds of ADD, add to this equation a very complex culture that is cultivating depression in young people, and factor in the divorce statistics which are leading to more and more dysfunctional families, the result is a very difficult situation. In working with children for over 30 years, I see a new child, one who is hurting, hard to help, difficult to diagnose, and requiring much restoration.

What it is:

Now let's take a look at what ADD and ADHD are. Basically, both involve neurotransmitter dysfunctions. In other words there are two points in the brain that do not connect. Let's look at two illustrations to better understand this. First of all, think of the brain as a bazillion dots. Learning is simply connecting those dots. With ADD and ADHD, there are some areas of the brain, such as those that regulate behavior, that simply do not connect. In those cases, medication becomes the chemical that makes the syntax operate. However, with medications it's important that the doctors prescribing them do so with great wisdom and experience.

Have you ever walked into a room to get something and you can't remember why you are there? How do you feel at that precise moment? Kind of stupid, huh? We all do. If I got in your face and said, "What do you mean you can't remember? Did you remember when you walked into the room? Well then, you should remember now!" would that help you remember? Of course not. It would make matters worse. You already felt stupid and this response only compounds it.

Dear teachers with HEART, this is a glimpse of what it feels like to be affected by ADD or ADHD. One moment you have it and the next moment you don't. The neurotransmitters simply disconnect for a second. The next time you are feeling frustrated with a child who has ADD or ADHD, remember how it felt to walk into a room and forget your purpose there. Doesn't that foster a more Christlike compassion? Love the child, encourage him, and he will learn.

ADD & ADHD: A Closer Look

The terms ADD and ADHD are common in the education world. Since the abilities to pay attention to the material being presented, and to sit still are so critical to good learning, the teacher needs to be aware of students with ADD and ADHD.

Sometimes students with ADD and ADHD are discussed as though they are not in the learning disability category. Medically, that is probably correct. However, the basic similarity between a student with a learning disability and a student with ADD or ADHD is simple. Neither can pay attention to a task and both exhibit a lot of meaningless movement. If the student has ADD, he is less hyperactive and impulsive. The diagnostic criteria for ADD and ADHD are in the *Diagnostic and Statistical Manual of Mental Disorders* (DSM–IV). The DSM outlines the symptoms of inattention, hyperactivity, and impulsiveness the child demonstrates in two settings (say school and home) by the time he is seven. These symptoms are not a part of any other disorder or problem.

Characteristics of students with learning disabilities
- attention deficits
- hyperactivity
- memory deficits
- perceptual deficits
- cognitive deficits
- motor and coordination difficulties (fine and gross skills are often poor)

- general orientation (may have trouble distinguishing between left and right)
- emotional liability (may cry when laughing is more appropriate
- may be immature for his age

If I had a learning disability, here is what I would want my teacher to know about me:
- I am trying to sit still.
- I can't keep my mind on one subject very long.
- A noise outside will distract me.
- I don't always pick up on cues about how you are feeling.
- I can be impulsive. Often I do something and then think about it.
- I try to listen, but my mind wanders.
- I don't always remember.
- I lose my belongings.
- In my mind, one and one do not always equal two.
- Often I feel stupid.
- I am really a nice person trying to learn and stay focused.
- I get frustrated.

Because students with learning disabilities make up the largest disability group served by special education in America (more than 50 percent), it is very likely that they will attend your class.

Excerpt from *Exceptional Teaching* by Jim Pierson. Standard Publishing, 2002.

Creating the Best Learning Environment

The best learning environments, of course, are those in which all four learning modalities are in place. If a child can use all four learning modalities simultaneously, learning is maximized. As teachers, we can do much to facilitate the learning process by teaching to all four modalities. The following chart offers suggestions for what teachers can provide in the classroom to incorporate all four:

VISUAL	AUDITORY	TACTILE	KINESTHETIC
• Ads	• Audio recordings	• Collections	• Acting things out
• Collages	• Books read aloud or on tape	• Composing music	• Active learning
• Coloring pictures	• Debates	• Dioramas	• Animated songs
• Designs or diagrams	• Dramas	• Finger plays	• Dance
• Films	• Interviews	• Flip charts	• Demonstrations
• Flannelgraph	• Limericks or riddles	• Hands-on learning	• Dramatizations
• Flow charts	• Music	• How-to books	• Experiments
• Graphic organizers	• Oral reports	• Jigsaw puzzles	• Field trips
• Hidden pictures in a scene	• Press conferences	• Manipulatives	• Games
• Maps & murals	• Questions	• Mobiles	• Inventions
• Portfolios & posters	• Readers' theatres	• Models	• Learning centers
• Storyboard lessons	• Rhymes	• Papier-mâché	• Puppet shows
• Transparency talks	• Role playing	• Pop-up books	• Role playing
• Videos & visuals	• Speeches	• Sculptures	• Simulation games
• Web sites & Web designs	• Teaching the lesson (themselves)	• Technology	• Skits

When preparing your next lesson, list three things you've planned for each of the four learning modalities to ensure you're planning for each learning style.

Understanding Learning Modalities

Answer the following questions to review the information in this chapter and to gain a better understanding of the learning modalities.

1. The modalities are the sensory gates through which we take in information. Are students one or the other, or combinations of all four?

2. What are three characteristics of a visual learner?
-
-
-

3. How can you spot visual learners in a classroom?

4. Name some visual learners in your classroom along with the specific visual characteristics that most define each learner.

5. What are three characteristics of an auditory learner?
-
-
-

6. How can you spot auditory learners in a classroom?

7. Name some auditory learners in your classroom along with the specific auditory characteristics that most define each learner.

8. What are three characteristics of a tactile learner?
-
-
-

9. How can you spot tactile learners in a classroom?

10. Name some tactile learners in your classroom along with the specific tactile characteristics that most define each learner.

11. What are three characteristics of a kinesthetic learner?
-
-
-

12. How can you spot kinesthetic learners in a classroom?

13. Name some kinesthetic learners in your classroom along with the specific kinesthetic characteristics most define each learner.

14. What way(s) do you best take in information? How do you think this impacts your teaching? What are some ways that you may need to step outside of your own learning modality?

Cherishing and Challenging Each Learning Modality

Fill in the appropriate spaces below. Then review the definitions and descriptions of how to appropriately cherish and challenge your students.

_____ Learners:

How to Cherish:
- Communicate through body language—a smile speaks volumes.
- Send various forms of communication (note cards, written encouragement, stickers, and so on).
- Provide a chart where the child can keep track of what she has achieved. Have a basket of stickers for the child to choose from. A word to the wise, even older children like stickers. It never ceases to amaze me!

How to Challenge:
- Use improvement charts to track behavior and accomplishments.
- Use written notes to encourage improved behavior or effort.
- Speak their language using terms like, "I see you trying harder."

_____ Learners:

How to Cherish:
- Remind them of how much you care by telling them!
- Watch how you use your tone of voice—displeasure in tone can signal these learners to shut down.
- Use music, rhymes, or raps to reinforce lessons and rules.

How to Challenge:
- Use verbal challenges like, "I know this is hard, but I believe you can do it."
- Use encouraging challenges like, "I see how you are trying to complete this project. I know you can do it!"
- Use a scriptural challenge. "What do you think Jesus would do in this situation? What does the Bible say about treating others as you would have them treat you?"

_____ Learners:

How to Cherish:
- Provide things to touch that are productive and related to what you are teaching.
- Provide manipulatives to facilitate learning.
- Provide tactile tools to enhance learning.

How to Challenge:
- Encourage comprehension by providing things to touch.
- Provide items to manipulate that will require these learners to work at a project with their hands.
- Teach tactile adaptive skills such as note taking, highlighting, and making note cards—encourage these learners to create their own tactile learning systems!

_____ Learners:

How to Cherish:
- Allow active learning.
- Provide positive opportunities to move and do.
- Channel energy into constructive activities.

How to Challenge:
- Affirm high energy levels and challenge channeling of energy in positive ways.
- Offer constructive outlets to help harness energy.
- Teach techniques and strategies for self-management.

Cherishing and Challenging Children to Fit God's Design of Their Learning Languages

A Teacher with HEART seeks ways to help each child learn according to how God created him.

Scripture: "Let the wise listen and add to their learning, and let the discerning get guidance" (Proverbs 1:5).

Teaching Objective: To find the learning language of each child in order to reach and teach him more effectively.

> **Our learning languages affect how we hear, process, store, and retrieve information.**

What Are Learning Languages?

We each learn in a unique way. In fact, we each have our own learning language. This learning language affects how we hear, process, store, and retrieve information. The modalities (seeing, hearing, talking, touching, and doing) are how we take in information. As we learned in the previous chapter, some learn best when they can see the lesson, others need to hear and talk about it, some children need to touch lesson-related items, and others need to do something with the information they're taking in. My goal in this chapter is to demystify the learning process so that every teacher can learn to apply these techniques to her teaching.

In this chapter I want to move to a deeper level of how information is processed. As discussed in Chapter 3, personalities are who we are in the flesh—they are who we are as people. If we view the learning process as peeling layers of an onion, the next layer would be the modalities (see Chapter 4), and that is how we take in information. As babies and young children, we simultaneously take in information via all of our sensory gates. We pick an item up, put it in our mouths, shake it, and hear it. As we get older, we become less multi-modality oriented. We begin to process more information through the brain wiring of our learning languages (or learning styles).

I would like to take some time to look at the different learning languages. Remember, we all have parts of all four. When we give a label to one of them it refers to a person's top score of the four different aspects of the learning languages format. This particular model is similar in some aspects to the 4MAT system developed by Bernice McCarthy.

The following factors determine our learning languages to a greater or lesser degree:
- How we relate to others and our environment
- What/how we observe our surroundings
- How we gather data
- What our intuition is prone to
- What hands-on learning experiences we have had
- How we have learned experientially
- How we analyze situations and people
- How/what we create

There are four different kinds of learners you may encounter in your classroom. Let's take a look at how they learn and then how to cherish and challenge them for Christ.

Dominic the Dynamic Learner

Who He Is:

Dominic is your leader. He is the visionary, the C.E.O. He thrives on activity and likes to do 16 things at once. He likes to get his hands on things, and much like Kinesthetic Kenan, he may often behave like a bull in a china closet. He charges and then aims. You don't ever have to motivate him because his switch is always ON!

Who He May Become:

He may have the gift of administration as he enjoys setting schedules, policies, and guidelines. He may, however, need to learn sensitivity. With this learning language, he can grow up to be a great leader because he is so production and goal oriented. However, you need to help him temper that drive with self-discipline. Pray for him to become a godly leader.

What He Thinks of You:

He sees the teacher as superfluous since he knows he could run things just fine. He responds well to you letting him be in charge of something. Like the choleric he only hears the words *in charge.* Since he loves activity you can put him in charge of most anything action-oriented, such as erasing the board or passing things out, and expect to get good results. He is your leader, so teach him wisely.

How to Identify Him in the Classroom:

There is no mistaking Dominic. He is much like Choleric Curtis. He comes into the room and immediately sizes up both you and the classroom. He looks around for something to do, someone to control (usually you), and a task to accomplish.

His strengths are that he
- thrives on activity
- displays abundant energy and drive
- loves "to do" and get things accomplished

His weaknesses are that he
- can be a discipline challenge
- has tendencies toward bullying
- thinks he is always right

To a dynamic learner the teacher is seen as superfluous. This learner knows he could run things just fine!

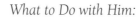

What to Do with Him:

Here are some helpful guidelines for managing a dynamic learner:

- Have lots of things for him to do that will keep him busy but calm. Puzzles are wonderful for him because he can touch and create while remaining relatively calm and quiet. This is much better than giving him an activity that would encourage him to be overly active. He will often finish his work quickly and need something else to do. Having things ready for him to do will provide much needed quiet for the classroom.

- Let him be in charge of something productive. Use those very words. Let it be something you choose, or give him two things to choose from. For example: "Dominic, you may be in charge of cleaning up the snack or collecting the crayons. Which do you choose?" Remember, he wants to have control, so give him limited control. Allow him to think he has made his own decision when, in reality, you have defined the parameters.

- Change the routine frequently because he is easily bored. Obviously certain routines are necessary for optimum classroom functioning. But find areas where you can provide change for him. He thrives on it.

- Remember that he is always thinking, *what can this become?* Provide a stimulating environment that he can explore to answer that question for himself. Again, have lots of things for him to touch.

How to Cherish:
- Give him tasks to be in charge of.
- Affirm his energy in a positive way: "I like the way you can get so much done!"
- Give him lots to do!

How to Challenge:
- Give him tasks to be in charge of.
- Leave tasks open-ended and let him figure out how to do them.
- Give him a time deadline—he loves to finish first!

Rachel the Relational Learner

Who She Is:

Relational Rachel functions best when she can talk about the lesson and relate to it. Thus, she is the sister to Sanguine Siena's personality. She loves to relate. She is very loving. She rules with her heart and is a people person.

Who She May Become:

She probably has the gift of mercy as she empathizes, gives, and loves. Or she may have the gift of giving as she gives generously to others. She may perhaps have the gift of exhortation as she ministers, comforts, and encourages.

When Relational Rachel grows up, she will do well in a people-oriented job. She may become a loving and warm teacher. Rachel has the heart to care and give to others, such as in a nursing vocation. With her excellent people skills, there are many opportunities to serve, love, and give that will open up for her.

What She Thinks of You:

The minute you say, "Let's talk about it," Rachel perks up. *Now you're speaking my language!* she seems to say. The truth is that she would talk in any language and uses her hands emphatically to make her point. Rachel wants to know why, and talking is the avenue through which she seeks her answers.

As a learner, Rachel learns best in a relational context. She is able to connect with the information if she has a positive relationship with the teacher. Both Relational Rachel and Sanguine Siena will either thrive or suffer based on their relationship with the teacher.

How to Identify Her in the Classroom:

You can recognize Relational Rachel immediately when she comes into the classroom. She will have someone with her, or a group of people if possible. She will be busy talking, laughing, and thoroughly enjoying herself. In class she is often talking instead of listening. If she is quiet, she is looking around at her friends trying different ways to connect. She is fun loving, quick to answer and volunteer for different tasks, and is eager to please.

If you ask her to stop talking she is quick to apologize and give you a big smile. Within five minutes, however, she may be talking again, and when you ask her to be quiet she may giggle and respond with, "Sorry, I forgot!" And yes, five minutes later she may be back to talking!

Remember Sanguine Siena? Her personality characteristics are much like the learning language characteristics of Relational Rachel. In fact it is very easy to get the two confused. Both are very extroverted,

> **Be careful! Relational learners will either thrive or suffer based on their relationship with the teacher.**

love people, and are more motivated to doing anything that involves people rather than tasks or paper work.

Her strengths are that she

- loves people and, as a result, has strong people skills
- is very creative
- is strongly intuitive

Her weaknesses are that she

- may ignore the paper tasks because she is so into the people scene
- may not apply herself if she does not relate to the teacher, because of her strong need for approval
- thinks if she apologizes, she is off the hook

What to Do with Her:

Here are some guidelines to better manage a relational learner:

- Give her lots of opportunities for discussion. In the classroom she will continually want to talk. She should be provided with positive opportunities to do so and then helped to understand when she needs to be quiet and listen or work. Since she is a nonstop talker, you may get tired of hearing her talk and begin to tune her out. However, if you schedule time to give her your complete attention, with the understanding that you cannot allow her to monopolize all of your time, you can begin to teach her some self-control in this area.
- Provide opportunities for her to encourage and serve others. She thrives on giving. She can make cards and cookies for shut-ins, or help another child with an activity. Encourage this beautiful gift she has because the world needs more of these people.
- Teach her self-control with her talking. As a relational learner she needs to learn that she cannot continually talk and ask questions. She has to learn when to be quiet and how to be a good listener.

How to Cherish:

- Take time to develop a relationship with her.
- Love, encourage, praise, and affirm her.
- Allow opportunities for subjective learning, such as discussions.

How to Challenge:

- Use her people strengths to develop leadership skills.
- Offer her creative outlets.
- Provide opportunities for subjective learning experiences.

> **The facial expression of an analytical learner seems to say, "Teach me more, but only the facts, please."**

Ali the Analytical Learner

Who He Is:

Analytical Ali, unlike Relational Rachel, does not particularly need to talk or relate. He wants the facts. He sees things in black and white. His key virtue is wisdom, and he rules with his head. He is conscientious, studious, analytical, and perfectionistic. His cousins may well be Melancholy Mei Li or Phlegmatic Patrick.

Who He May Become:

Analytical Ali may have the gift of teaching as he researches, analyzes, and seeks to teach the facts. He may grow up to be a good teacher of intellectual information or a research analyst, but he could become a workaholic to avoid interacting with people. Gently teach him people skills and remember that this is very difficult for him, so be patient.

What He Thinks of You:

Analytical Ali is a quieter child. He likes to observe others. He likes to study things and analyze them. He may be critical, but he doesn't accept criticism well. He may not participate in as much imaginary play as the other children because he is so factual. He may not have as many friends as Relational Rachel, but he is a most interesting child to teach.

How to Identify Him in the Classroom:

Analytical Ali is usually a quiet child. As a student he usually has a serious face with a look that seems to imply: *Teach me more, but only the facts, please.* He is generally a good student, gets his work done, loves research, prefers to work alone, and rarely needs help.

Some of his strengths are that he
- is a great student
- loves research
- thrives on facts, information, and teachers who know what they're talking about

Some of his weaknesses are that he
- can be aloof
- may be absentminded
- loves the abstract but often misses the relational component

What to Do with Him:

Here are some guidelines to better manage an analytical learner:

- Provide opportunities for him to discuss things in his comfort zone, which is the objective arena. Remember that Ali is not comfortable with discussing subjective issues, such as how he feels about something. Slowly help him to understand his feelings and then to express them. This will have to be taught, it does not come naturally for him.

  He feels things deeply but cannot articulate them with ease. Sometimes you have to give him the words that he does not possess spontaneously, in terms of relating to himself. For example, he could give you a letter-perfect definition of the word *depression* but could not verbalize how this could ever relate to his own experience. It is easy for him to acquire knowledge, but he cannot always apply it as wisdom to his personal situation.

- Provide Bible facts. Hold Bible drills and contests as well as other factual learning experiences for him. This is where he excels and where you can provide opportunities for him to shine.

- Develop a quiet, orderly environment that is well supplied with reference books such as Bible dictionaries or atlases. He does not like activity or discussion, he simply enjoys the process of acquiring more factual information. Therefore this learning language usually makes him a good student.

- Teach him people skills since he often does not have them spontaneously. He has to be taught how to relate factual information to real-life situations.

How to Cherish:
- Provide research opportunities.
- Provide facts and objective data.
- Answer his external questions: "Why?" and "How?"

How to Challenge:
- Give him theories to synthesize.
- Give him information beyond the basic lesson.
- Give him critical thinking assignments that go to a deeper level of understanding.

Sequential Shani

> **Sequential learners want you to be the teacher and not necessarily their friend.**

Shani the Sequential Learner

Who She Is:

Sequential Shani's thinking is logical and linear. She is a sequential thinker. She sees the details first and as she puts together the details she sees the patterns. Finally she sees the big picture. But for her to go from the details to the big picture, she must proceed in a very linear, sequential manner. She likes cause and effect relationships that are logical in their orientation.

Who She May Become:

Shani is often a serious child. She has a high need for order and predictability. She is often like an adult in a child's body. Her spiritual gifts may include administration and organization. When she grows up, she may lean toward a job that is more analytical in nature. She might become an engineer, accountant, manager or behind the scenes person in a ministry or business as she keeps things organized.

What She Thinks of You:

Sequential Shani wants you to be the teacher and not necessarily her friend. She likes schedules, scope and sequence charts, predictability, and punctuality. She wants the teacher to truly be the teacher and by that she wants you to stay in the role of the one who maintains order in the classroom.

Shani does not like when the classroom becomes too loud or doesn't stay on the schedule, or when the teacher doesn't maintain proper discipline. Shani may get a stomachache or headache if things aren't staying on task.

How to Identify Her in the Classroom:

Sequential Shani comes in quietly and goes to her place. She consistently does the right thing. You may notice her at first because she is so quiet and orderly and does not do anything to attract attention to herself.

Some of her strengths are that she is
- organized
- attentive
- responsible and mature

Some of her weaknesses are that she
- can be inflexible—she does not like when the classroom becomes too open-ended or when there is not a clear, definite plan
- has difficulty thinking outside the box
- may be impatient with other students who don't take learning seriously

What to Do with Her:

Here are some guidelines to better manage a sequential learner:

- Clearly define expectations for projects or assignments. She does well in the box of carefully communicated boundaries. Keep structure in the classroom through scheduling and discipline. These provide her with a sense that you know what you're doing.
- Offer objective learning experiences such as Bible drills and the memorization of factual information in which she can excel. She responds well to assignments like the following: make a Bible timeline showing the kings of the northern and southern kingdoms.
- Praise her for following the rules and obeying the directions. It frustrates her when she does follow the rules and others do not, and there are no apparent consequences for the non-rule followers. "I like the way Shani is raising her hand to speak and, therefore, I am going to call on Shani."
- The following are words in her learning language: list, categorize, graph, organize, memorize, plan, and sequence. Avoid open-ended projects, playing it by ear, and chaos.

How to Cherish:

- Provide structure—use a syllabus and/or a schedule.
- Define your expectations in detail.
- If you have to change the plan, give her warning and a reason.

How to Challenge:

- Provide opportunities for extra activities or seatwork.
- Give her projects to organize.
- Have her analyze and synthesize information by having her search for more evidence about a concept.

It is impossible to state rules that work for every child. Teaching must be approached on an individual basis.

As we look at the different ways that children learn, it is easy to see why teaching can be so difficult. Each child enters the world with a completely unique script and purpose. That is why it is impossible to state simplistic rules for teaching and expect them to work for every child. Teaching must be approached on an individual basis.

The Bible provides excellent guidelines for raising children to be godly adults, and we can benefit from the wisdom gained from God's Word. However, we must also remember to see each child as the unique creation that God intended him to be—specifically designed for God's ultimate purpose. Because God knows His purpose for each child, He is the best source of wisdom on how to teach that child. "If any of you lacks wisdom, he should ask God, who gives generously to all without finding fault, and it will be given to him" (James 1:5). Pray continually to be the teacher God needs you to be for each of your students.

Understanding Learning Languages

Answer the following questions to evaluate how you relate to the various learning languages of your students.

1. What learning modality (see Chapter 4) do you most relate to as an adult?
- Visual (You like to see it and have things written down.)
- Auditory (You need to hear and talk about it.)
- Tactile (You need to touch things.)
- Kinesthetic (You thrive on doing.)

2. Which learning language do you think best describes you? Why?
- Dynamic
- Relational
- Analytical
- Sequential

3. In what ways can you see that your learning modality and language come together to impact how you teach children?

4. Match each of the four learning languages to a specific student in your classroom.

5. How can you best work with your students to facilitate their learning language needs?

6. Do you think your students' learning needs are being met in your classroom environment? If not, what can you do to facilitate the process?

7. Complete the chart on the following page listing additional ways you can effectively cherish and challenge each of the different learning languages present in your classroom.

Cherishing and Challenging Each Learning Languages

Fill in the chart below, listing ways you can more effectively cherish and challenge the students you teach, according to their learning modalities.

Dynamic Learners

Ways to cherish more effectively
-
-
-

Ways to challenge more effectively
-
-
-

Learns best with
-
-
-

Teach with
-
-
-

Relational Learners

Ways to cherish more effectively
-
-
-

Ways to challenge more effectively
-
-
-

Learns best with
-
-
-

Teach with
-
-
-

Analytical Learners

Ways to cherish more effectively
-
-
-

Ways to challenge more effectively
-
-
-

Learns best with
-
-
-

Teach with
-
-
-

Sequential Learners

Ways to cherish more effectively
-
-
-

Ways to challenge more effectively
-
-
-

Learns best with
-
-
-

Teach with
-
-
-

A Closer Look at Learning Languages

Match each learning language to its description below and fill in the blanks accordingly. Then review the characteristics, gifts, and areas of improvement for each learning language, as well as how these learners relate to their teachers.

_____ learners . . .

- thrive on activity and are much like Kinesthetic Kenan—their switches are always ON!
- may have the gift of administration and enjoy setting schedules.
- need to learn to temper their goal oriented drive with sensitivity and self-discipline.
- see the teacher as superfluous and only hear the words *in charge.*

_____ learners . . .

- do not particularly need to talk or relate and are closely related to Melancholy Mei Li or Phlegmatic Patrick—they see things in black and white.
- may have the gift of teaching as they research and analyze the facts.
- need to be gently encouraged to build people skills and not to use work as a way of avoiding interaction with others.
- may seem critical but do not accept criticism well.

_____ learners . . .

- function best when they can talk about the lesson and are closely related to Sanguine Siena—they rule with their hearts!
- may have the gift of mercy as they empathize easily with others.
- need to be encouraged to apply themselves to tasks that are not as people oriented as they are.
- will either thrive or suffer based on how they relate to the teacher.

_____ learners . . .

- see the details first and look for the patterns.
- may have the gifts of administration and organization as they display a high need for order and predictability.
- need to be encouraged to be flexible and to remain patient with other students who don't take learning as seriously.
- want the teacher to remain in the teacher role and not try to be their friend.

Chapter 6

Cherishing and Challenging Children Through Multiple Intelligences and Faith Development

A Teacher with HEART sees all truth as God's truth and uses research to learn ways to better cherish and challenge each student more effectively. A teacher with HEART identifies the giftedness God has placed in each child and seeks to teach in a way that brings out each unique gift.

Scripture: "But each man has his own gift from God; one has this gift, another has that" (1 Corinthians 7:7).

Teaching Objective: To find relevant ways to teach to the God-given giftedness of each child.

Multiple Intelligences

Understanding Multiple Intelligences

Dr. Howard Gardner presented the concept of Multiple Intelligences in the 80s in his prize-winning book, *Frames of Mind* (Gardner 1985). While it was widely embraced at first, additional brain research has since provided us with more objective data to understand how children learn. However, I am presenting Dr. Gardner's research in this book as a framework of information to support the premise that each child is uniquely created by God for His purpose. Let us use the premise of Multiple Intelligences to better understand the differences in each child.

When it first came out, Ernest Boyer of the Carnegie Foundation for the Advancement of Teaching referred to this model of intelligence as the most exciting work currently being done in the field of learning. Gardner's theory of Multiple Intelligences provides a solid foundation upon which to identify and develop a broad spectrum of abilities within each child. Gardner's model gives us a way of looking at the complete picture of a learner's potential so that neglected abilities will be honored and developed.

Dr. Gardner identified seven types of intelligence. We all use all seven but in different proportions. The seven are as follows:

Linguistic Intelligence: Word Smart

These children have highly developed auditory skills and are gifted at language. They like to write, tell stories, read, spell, and play word games. They love rhymes, tongue twisters, crossword puzzles, and can even remember names, dates, and trivia easily.

Logical/Mathematical: Logic Smart

These children are capable of highly abstract forms of logical thinking. They love computers, chess, logic puzzles, working out math problems in their heads, and devising ways to find answers to questions they don't understand.

Spatial Intelligence: Picture Smart

These children think in images or pictures. They love to do art projects, can read maps and charts easily, seem to know where everything is, and often daydream. They like movies, slides, photos, and jigsaw puzzles.

Musical Intelligence: Music Smart

These children often sing or hum while doing other activities. They love to sing, play instruments, have music on while studying, collect tapes or CD's, and can tell you when a note is off-key. They respond well to music playing in the background. This is the intelligence that emerges at the youngest age.

Bodily Kinesthetic: Body Smart

These children are constantly on the move. They process knowledge through bodily sensations and get gut feelings about things. They are gifted at physical activities such as fixing things, playing sports, dancing, sewing, and crafts. They like to touch people when talking to them and often enjoy scary amusement park rides.

Interpersonal Intelligence: People Smart

These children understand people. They are frequently leaders and can organize and communicate well. They have a lot of friends, socialize well, and are empathetic and able to mediate relationships well.

Intrapersonal Intelligence: Self-Smart

These children have strong personalities but shy away from group activities. They bloom best alone. They may keep a diary, have hobbies, and often live in a private world. They have a deep sense of self-confidence and may display a strong sense of independence or seem strong willed.

Dr. Thomas Armstrong has developed this concept further in his writings, which include, *In Their Own Way* (Armstrong 1987) from which much of this information is taken. He adds another intelligence, which is Spiritual or Moral Smart. These children are gifted in a special way at dealing with spiritual and moral issues. They gravitate easily toward doing what is right and love Scripture and prayer.

Dr. Armstrong offers practical suggestions for how to teach anything in these seven different intelligences. Another resource that is helpful in providing excellent suggestions on teaching to the different intelligences is *Seven Ways of Teaching: The Artistry of Teaching With Multiple Intelligences* written by David Lazear (1991).

Listed below are some examples of how teachers can help their students learn using their natural giftedness.

- Linguistic learners: use books, oral presentations, writing, and make tapes.
- Logical math learners: collect statistics about the lesson and offer additional research options.
- Spatial learners: use charts and pictures, or make charts and pictures.
- Kinesthetic learners: allow moving, doing, touching, building, working with manipulatives, and working while seated on the floor or while standing.
- Musical learners: use music to work or teach by, and put information that needs to be memorized to music.

- Interpersonal learners: allow study buddies, work in groups, and allow students to share ideas with one another.
- Intrapersonal learners: create a place for children to work alone and to do independent projects.

One of the main purposes of this book is to help you see each of your students as God has intended them to be for His purpose. I want you to find ways to cherish and challenge each of them more effectively. The following chart will help you organize these different intelligences in order to best reach and teach your students.

For the purposes of this book, I have added two additional intelligences to this chart. One is Naturalistic Intelligence (which Dr. Gardner added to his list at a later time) and the other includes the development of Faith and Moral Reasoning (which will be discussed later in this chapter).

Multiple Intelligences and Faith Development

Cherishing and Challenging Each Intelligence

Intelligence	Smart	How to Cherish	How to Challenge
Linguistic	Word Smart	Allow opportunities for these children to communicate verbally, or through writing, in order to express themselves or their responses to the lesson.	Use writing activities. Use different languages for parts of a lesson (i.e. memory verses). Provide speaking opportunities.
Logical/ Mathematical	Logic Smart	Affirm their ability to see things objectively, and allow them to use this ability in class through puzzles and problem solving activities. Keep in mind that they enjoy math, science, statistics, accounting, or any subject that is logical and linear.	Encourage students to analyze challenging situations/issues. Provide organizational projects. Give projects that show a logical cause and effect relationship.
Spatial	Picture Smart	Affirm their giftedness. These children are very bright but the level of their intellect may not be measurable by the same standards used for other intelligences.	Provide creative outlets through painting. Allow them to help with decorating projects. Let them incorporate graphs or charts into the lesson—let them create their own!
Musical	Music Smart	Praise their musical gifts and allow them to express their ideas musically. Let them listen to music as they work.	Encourage them to sing or play an instrument. Help them write songs (or psalms). Let them find and teach songs that correlate with the lesson being taught.
Bodily Kinesthetic	Body Smart	This child's valuable intelligence may not be measurable by the same standards used for other children. Affirm where their giftedness manifests and encourage them in those areas!	Give them opportunities to invent activities or act out motions that correlate with the lesson. Encourage them to use their gift of creativity. Use sports and games to help them relate to the lesson and to other children.

Cherishing and Challenging Each Intelligence (Continued)

Intelligence	Smart	How to Cherish	How to Challenge
Interpersonal	People Smart	Praise their people skills and let them lead and minister through their people gifts. Tell them often how much you appreciate them.	Provide service opportunities. Encourage them to help you in motivating other children toward a goal or completing a task. Stretch their communication skills—allow them to be discussion leaders.
Intrapersonal	Self Smart	Allow them the freedom to be who they are, which may often be a loner. Praise them for their understanding of self and spend one-on-one time with them.	Provide behind the scenes opportunities for these children. Encourage them to mentor others. Challenge them to organize the details of a project.
Naturalistic	Nature Smart	Praise them for their ability to perceive patterns in God's creation. Allow them opportunities to use their gifts to inspire others to appreciate creation in the same way.	Let them organize indoor or outdoor gardening projects. Encourage them to suggest lesson-related outdoors activities. Have them set up a nature center for the classroom.
Spiritual Gift of Faith Development	Faith Gift (The ability to perceive and receive that which is not seen)	The faith of children is so pure. Let's praise it! Encourage children to pray individually as well as to lead the class in prayer time.	Encourage children to pray beyond their familiar world such as their families and friends. Create a Faith Tree or Wall (See Chapter 14). Have them research people who have lived lives that reflect a foundation of faith and synthesize the common denominators.
Moral Reasoning	Moral Gift (The ability to discern right from wrong)	Praise children who recognize right from wrong and choose right! This is especially important when the decision was difficult or cost them something.	Challenge kids to bring current issues to class for discussion. Encourage them to develop their own answers to tough issues before giving them the right answer. For older students, hold debates on moral issues to help train them in moral discernment.

Children function more positively today when they feel hopeful about tomorrow.

As we prepare our students for a Christian life, let us help them recognize their God-given intelligences. For all of us, when we feel smart we feel energized, encouraged, and empowered. Some students don't do well in school and may have the impression that life will be just like their school experiences. They may feel discouraged and assume that they will never succeed in life. When we help them identify and utilize their gifts, we give them a window to see their future. They will function more positively today when they feel hopeful about tomorrow. It is sad to see children drifting seemingly without hope. Let's equip them for their future by empowering them now!

Students feel encouraged, energized, and empowered when we give them tools to see themselves as God has created them to be for His purpose. From this base of understanding, we can show them how their gifts can be used for a future profession. It gives our students focus and helps them to appreciate the education they are receiving today when they know it will help prepare them for their future. The work becomes meaningful and purposeful and not a waste of their time, which is how many students perceive educational experiences.

The following chart details each intelligence with information about what these intelligences may lead to in a child's future.

Multiple Intelligences and Faith Development

Looking Ahead

Intelligence	Skills to Incorporate		Future Possibilities	
Word Smart (Linguistic)	• Communicating • Debating • Speaking foreign languages	• Writing	• Author • Language teacher • Lawyer	• Missionary • Pastor • Teacher
Logic Smart (Logical/Mathematical)	• Analyzing • Classifying • Practicing math skills	• Sequencing • Systematizing • Using statistics	• Accountant • Business manager • Computer analyst	• Insurance statistician • Math teacher • Technician
Picture Smart (Spacial)	• Decorating • Designing • Graphing	• Illustrating • Mapping • Painting	• Architect • Artist • Cartographer • Computer graphic designer	• Decorator • Designer • Illustrator • Planner • Sculptor
Music Smart (Musical)	• Composing music • Playing instruments	• Singing	• Music teacher • Singer/musician	• Song writer
Body Smart (Kinesthetic)	• Building • Creating • Dancing • Multitasking	• Playing athletic games • Sorting	• Athlete • Construction worker • Dancer	• Doctor • Inventor • Nurse • Pilot
People Smart (Interpersonal)	• Communicating • Counseling • Motivating	• Serving • Tutoring	• Coach • Counselor • Manager • Pastor • Politician • Public relations worker	• Public speaker • Sales representative • Teacher

Looking Ahead (Continued)

Intelligence	Skills to Incorporate		Future Possibilities	
Self Smart (Intrapersonal)	• Appraising • Evaluating • Internally analyzing	• Organizing • Reflecting • Working alone	• Appraiser • Author • Behind-the-scenes worker • Counselor	• Psychologist • Systems analylist • Theologian
Nature Smart (Naturalistic)	• Gardening • Completing outdoor projects • Working with animals		• Gardening specialist • Parks & recreation manager • Veterinarian	
Faith Development	• Leading the class • Planning new missions • Setting goals		• Entrepreneur • Missionary • Pastor	
Moral Reasoning	• Organizing missions events • Organizing service events • Organizing youth events		• Counselor • Judge	• Pastor • Teacher

Faith Development

Faith is the foundation of everything in our walk with the Lord. It is imperative that we help our students to understand the development of faith in their lives. While the Bible is the primary source of our faith building training, we have a rich resource of research in this area to draw on as well.

James Fowler studied the work of Jean Piaget, Erik Erickson, and Lawrence Kohlberg. From his studies he began his own research of faith development. Fowler has made the study of faith the focus of his life's work. As he examined the process of faith development, he identified characteristics of the process that are common among persons of various religions including Christianity, Judaism, Islam, and secular humanism. Fowler examined the faith of children, youth, and adults and identified specific changes in faith as it is progressed (Fowler 1991). Fowler offered a three-part definition of faith. Fowler's views of faith are that it:

- Is a dynamic pattern of personal trust in and loyalty to a center or centers of value.
- Involves trust in and loyalty to images and realities of power.
- Involves trust in and loyalty to a shared master's story or core story.

Trust and loyalty are the foundation—the threads woven through all dimensions of faith. Without faith, life is empty and meaningless. God created human beings with the capacity and the deep need for faith (Fowler 1989).

Fowler believed that there are stages in faith development for children. Fowler's understanding of primal faith came from Erickson's description of the first life crisis: trust versus mistrust. Primal faith is a basic building block that forms trust in young children. He believed that as children are cherished, it sets the stage for faith to grow. What a profound impact this truth can have on our ministry!

Fowler also believed that memories formed while children are young contribute to their faith development as well. Brain research has taught us that in order for memories to move from short-term to long-term there must be an emotional component. Let us pray that the memories children have are a result of positive rather than negative emotions. Fowler also stated that rituals can help form positive memories in children. What power we can add to our students' faith by providing rituals of our faith.

In Hebrews 11 we learn that it was demonstrations of faith that have formed the great lessons that we continue to pass from

> We have a rich resource of research to drawn on as we study faith development.

generation to generation. These stories are now a part of our own faith heritage.

Fowler states that it is in our early years that the basic foundation of faith is constructed. What an enormous responsibility we have been given to instill in children the basic rituals of our faith, as well as a strong sense of God's loving care at a young age.

Moral Development

In the 1930s, Piaget began to study the moral development of children. During this study he theorized that children are moral philosophers who struggle with good and evil, understanding and applying rules. Lawrence Kohlberg discovered the works of Piaget and building on the work, continued to study moral development.

Piaget and Kohlberg discovered that when children are faced with moral decisions, their thought processes differ from the moral reasoning of most adults. Insights from Piaget and Kohlberg help us understand what is going on inside of children as they deal with the moral challenges of everyday life. From extensive research, Kohlberg identified three levels of moral reasoning (Kohlberg 1981).

Kohlberg's levels of moral reasoning provide clearly delineated time periods during which it is possible to understand how children develop moral reasoning. These include:

- Level One—Pre-Conventional:
  At this stage children are aware of some of the rules in their world, but their attention is focused on the pleasure related to a deed, not on the moral implications. The reasoning behind their actions is to gain a reward or to avoid punishment. In other words, their moral reasoning comes from an authority figure and is not intrinsic.

- Level Two—Conventional:
  Children at this level live in accordance to the moral standards of their friends and the world around them. Children begin to set up simple categories in their minds that say right is what good people do and wrong is what bad people do. At this level children begin to see God as someone to be valued because He loves them. Jesus is the key model for students at this level.

- Level Three—Post-Conventional:
  According to moral reasoning at this level, doing what is right is part of living by moral principles, and wrong is defined as anything that the violates these principles. Children at this level want to meet the expectations of their family, friends, and

> **Piaget theorized that children are moral philosophers who struggle with good and evil and with rules.**

society. To them, this is more important than the immediate results of an action. At Level Three children begin to understand that people have value and that caring for others is as important as caring for self.

Robert Coles, child psychologist, well-known author, and professor at Harvard University has also spent time studying children and their moral development. Coles' method was formed over several years of getting to know children in depth. Out of these encounters, he developed a profound respect for the moral courage in children, particularly those who have lived with tragedy and pain. As he read Piaget and Kohlberg, he was continually reminded of the moral behavior of some of the children he studied whose actions seemed to be much beyond what the developmentalist believed possible in childhood. Coles went to the children, listened to them, and reflected upon his encounters in his book, *The Moral Life of Children* (Coles 1987). Coles cautions against a narrow, simplistic understanding of moral bodies. His work is a reminder that though we can be guided by insights from Erickson, Piaget, and Kohlberg on ways in which teachers can facilitate the development of children, we must never assume that we control the process. There is great mystery in each child's becoming and in each child's marvelous potential that is strengthened in a vital faith community.

Biblical stories play an important role in an elementary child's search for answers. Coles found that children relate the experiences of biblical characters to the events in their own lives. As children think about the stories, they see themselves in the biblical characters, and they see God working as they relate to these characters. Certain stories inspire children and draw them to reflect on life's meaning and on God.

As Coles talked with Christian children, he was impressed by how important Jesus was to them. He sensed that in a special way they sought Jesus as their Savior. Children identified with Him because He had been a child just as they are. His life had a purpose and that interested children who wondered about their own futures. For many children Jesus was far more than an historical figure. When children needed help to behave or with their personal problems, they often turned to Jesus to guide them. Jesus can be very real to older children.

Moral development is an important lifelong journey for all of us. But it is important that that we teach faith concepts to children in light of what is developmentally appropriate. In light of our culture it becomes even more important that we "Train a child in

> That Jesus was a child whose life held purpose interests children who wonder about their own futures.

We want children to develop a heart for others, live a life of service, and love others as themselves.

the way he should go, and when he is old he will not turn from it" (Proverbs 22:6). We want our students to go beyond the pre-conventional level to the post-conventional level so that they will have developed a heart for others, will live a life of service wherever God has placed them, and love their neighbors as themselves (Luke 10:27). As teachers with HEART, let us take time to find out where our students currently are in this process so that we may help them to move onward and upward.

Multiple Intelligences and Faith Development

A Closer Look at Multiple Intelligences

Answer the following questions to review the research on multiple intelligences:

1. In what activities can we engage our learners that will help us to identify what their areas of giftedness may be?

2. What do you think your intelligences and gifts are?

3. When did you first realize you had those gifts?

4. How are you using them for God's kingdom?

5. What are James Fowler's levels of faith development in children?

6. How can you see those demonstrated in the children you teach?

7. How can you help develop them further?

8. Complete the chart below to review Kohlberg's levels and to identify observable signs of these levels in your students:

	Level One:	**Level Two:**	**Level Three:**
Definition			
Source of Authority			
How do they respond to this source of authority? At home? At church? At school?			

Multiple Intelligences and Faith Development

How to Cherish and Challenge Each Intelligence

Complete the following chart to review the details of cherishing and challenging each intelligence:

Intelligence	Smart	How to Cherish	How to Challenge
Linguistic	Word Smart	Allow them to communicate _____ or through _____ to express themselves.	• • •
Logical/ Mathematical			• • Provide organizational projects. •
Spatial	P_____ Smart		• • •
Musical		Praise their _____ gifts and allow them to express their _____ musically. Let them _____ to music.	• • •
Bodily Kinesthetic			• • • Use sports and games to help them relate.

Multiple Intelligences and Faith Development

How to Cherish and Challenge Each Intelligence (Continued)

Intelligence	Smart	How to Cherish	How to Challenge
Interpersonal			• Provide service opportunities. • •
Intrapersonal	Self Smart		• • •
Naturalistic		Praise them for their ability to perceive _____ in _____ _____.	• • •
Spiritual Gift of Faith Development			• Encourage children to pray beyond their world • •
Moral Reasoning	Morally Smart		• • •

Cherishing and Challenging Children to Fit God's Design of Their Brain Orientation

A Teacher with HEART recognizes that all truth is God's truth and strives to learn from the wisdom of others.

Scripture: "But as for you, continue in what you have learned and have become convinced of, because you know those from whom you learned it, and how from infancy you have known the holy Scriptures, which are able to make you wise for salvation through faith in Christ Jesus" (2 Timothy 3:14, 15).

Teaching Objective: To see God's truth in the collective wisdom of various researchers and to apply this wisdom in the Christian classroom.

The world of brain research is an exciting dimension. The teacher with HEART will use this amazing information to enhance the teaching process. There is so much information on the market today, and it can be overwhelming. It is my heart's desire to provide practical nuggets of information and to help you digest and apply them to your teaching. I want to provide some brief facts and then supportive practical information to help you in your journey to reach children and to shape young hearts with God's Word.

Before we examine current research on this topic, let us again look to one of the pioneers of child development research—Jean Piaget. Through some of the conclusions of his research, we will learn how we can cherish and challenge our students more effectively.

Piaget believed that all children progress through the developmental stages in the same order. The skills developed at one stage form the foundation for further development in the next stage. For decades the results of this research have been used by educators to enhance physical, social, and emotional learning. Why should we not utilize this valuable information to teach God's Word more effectively? As we examine each stage, we will see how this research is useful in preparing classroom environments and learning experiences for children, in order to maximize their spiritual learning.

Sensorimotor/Practical Intelligence

The first stage is identified as the Sensorimotor, or Practical Intelligence, stage and occurs from birth to ages 1 to 2. Piaget states that during this stage a baby's actions are their thoughts, and in their thoughts they slowly begin to connect cause and effect to obtain desired results.

A baby's first move is by accident and the result of a simple reflex action. When a baby or toddler sees a positive response too their actions, they repeat them, thus discovering the first level of cause and effect. Babies and toddlers continue to learn through sensory channels (see, smell, taste, hear, and touch) until their verbal skills begin to develop. At the beginning when a baby drops a toy, they do not search for it because they think since it cannot be seen, it does not exist. As they begin to develop and realize that objects can exist without being seen, their anxiety about Mom and Dad dropping them off at the nursery or with a babysitter ceases to be as intense. Teachers can use games such as Peek-a-Boo to help children in this stage see the fun in things appearing and disappearing.

In our church nurseries, childcare programs, Mother's day out events, etc., it is essential that we demonstrate the love of Jesus Christ to each baby and toddler. In this first stage we are able to plant seeds that teach them that Jesus loves them and that church is a safe and loving environment. We can talk to them and sing to them about Jesus. We can hold them and comfort them. Our actions at this stage speak volumes as we hold them, feed them, change their diapers, and take care of them while their parents are away.

Preoperational/Intuitive

As children learn to walk and talk they move into the next stage. The Preoperational, or Intuitive, stage begins between ages 1 and 2 and lasts until age 7 or 8. During this stage of development, children amaze both parents and teachers. There is no other stage or age at which a person learns at such a rapid rate. Preschoolers are the brightest people on the planet and certainly have the most energy. It is unfortunate that they lack wisdom, or we could let them take care of everything.

If you have ever observed preschool children, especially around age 4, you notice that they tend to talk continually. They see inanimate objects as if they were alive and able to carry on a continuous, collective monologue. Children in this stage have an egocentric perspective. They assume that everyone thinks as they do. According to Piaget, they think intuitively rather than logically. Research shows that they do not connect the dots in a logical sequence, however, when presented with sensory information in an orderly fashion, they seemingly do connect the dots. Their learning is sensorimotor and this leads to them knowing.

Volumes of sensory information are coming in via the senses. A young child needs to create a memory file cabinet for this information in order to retrieve it. As teachers we can help them to order these many multisensory experiences by providing names, labels, and categories. After hearing *ball*, touching *ball*, tasting *ball*, and throwing *ball*, they begin to know what a ball is. As language develops they will begin to know what a red ball is, a big ball, a football, etc.

Piaget's research reveals that young children are perception bound. This means that they center on one concept and become completely absorbed in it. Dr. Maria Montessori also observed this unique quality of young children to completely absorb their surroundings. Dr. Montessori was the first woman physician in Italy. She studied (including Piaget's work) and worked with children.

> **Your actions speak volumes to children from birth to age 2.**

She wrote books based upon her ministry with children including *The Absorbent Mind* (1980) and *The Secret of Childhood* (1966). She writes of the profound ability of a young child from birth to age 6 to completely absorb the language, culture, and customs of their world, and reflect them back. This truly is one of the secrets of childhood—the absorbent mind.

Children at this stage seemingly teach themselves as they explore, discuss, create, and absorb their environment. As a teacher with HEART, recognize this profound stage and lay a banquet of sensory experiences before children from which they can learn. Help children organize the vast amounts of information they absorb so that they can effectively access their new knowledge.

Children at this second stage continually ask questions. They live in the present and cannot perceive the past or the future. For example, as I was teaching a lesson on Noah, one of the children asked, "Why didn't Noah take Jesus on the ark"? Great question! In order to cherish and challenge children in our teaching, we must patiently answer the myriad of questions children ask in their efforts to integrate volumes of information. Assisting children in successfully accomplishing this task helps to move them into the third stage.

Concrete/Intellectual Operations

Concrete Operations, or Concrete Intellectual Operations, is the third stage and begins between ages 7 and 8 and lasts until age 11 or 12. WOW! Here we find a big developmental breakthrough as children begin to move from thinking intuitively to thinking logically. Children are now able to begin considering, connecting, and coordinating different perspectives. They can also begin to understand the concept of time and history because they now possess the skill of reversible thinking. They can look back!

History is *His*-story. History reveals the providential hand of God as He works through people and events to carry out His plan.

Kohlberg and Piaget state, "during this period of concrete operations, children learn to place events in sequential order with a duration of time inserted between them and that a timeline would provide a picture of the sequential ordering" (Piaget 1967). Thus, history begins to come alive and have relevance for this day and time. Students begin to see that actions have consequences and that this concept applies to their actions as well.

The world of child development is so exciting. I have always loved children. I love to observe children. They never cease to

> **Children ages 2 to 8 seem to teach themselves. Lay a banquet of sensory experiences before them.**

amaze me! I am thankful that the Lord has allowed me to work with children for over 30 years as a teacher, principal, minister to children, and headmaster. While I have not provided a rich research base such as what is provided by Piaget, Montessori, Erickson, and Kohlberg, I do have consistent views about children that have developed through my years of experience.

I believe passionately that we must teach children in the ways they learn best. As teachers with HEART, we must provide learning environments that are consistent with the research provided for us in order to help children develop to their full potential at each developmental stage. I may be preaching to the choir, but I must communicate this point. Nowhere, in anyone's research, does it say that children learn best doing work sheets all day, day after day. Yet if you walk into most classrooms, that is often what you will find. A teacher with HEART adapts to the students' developmental stages and prepares lessons with the needs of the students in mind.

Let's take a moment to look into the world of current brain research. The following factors are rooted in the results of brain development research and dramatically affect the learning process for children. A teacher with HEART will benefit from these research results and apply this information to the classroom experience in order to maximize learning!

There is so much research on the market right now and it can be overwhelming as you begin the journey to see what is available. You may be asking how teachers in the Christian classroom can utilize this information to enhance their teaching? I will offer some practical suggestions in the following section. I have also listed some resources in the bibliography that are reader friendly. I heartily recommend books by Eric Jensen such as *Teaching with the Brain in Mind* (1998).

> **Nowhere, in anyone's research, does it say that children learn best by doing work sheets all day!**

ABC's of Brain Development

ARTS: Studying the arts enhances brain connections, increases language development, boosts reading readiness, and encourages social development. In addition, students excel and learn better in all areas when the arts are incorporated.

ATTENTION: Anything that captures students' attention and gets their minds engaged has the potential to produce learning. If there is no attention and engagement, learning will not take place. A teacher can provide a puppet for younger children to help grab their attention. Similarly, a hands-on activity to introduce a concept works for students of all ages. The teacher can also dress in a way that represents the lesson in order to initiate questions and immediate interest. These are just a few ways to grab the attention of your students.

BALANCE: Helping students learn to use both hemispheres of the brain in a balanced manner is one of the many goals of teaching. As we come to better understand our students and how they learn, we are better able to employ a learning style approach to teaching, which helps students to make brain connections more effectively.

BRAIN DEVELOPMENT: Stages of brain development are especially critical in the early years. Take advantage of this learning time by creating exciting, multisensory learning environments for young children.

CHOICES: The corpus callosum is made up of 250 million nerve fibers that enable connections in the brain to transfer information from the left hemisphere to the right hemisphere. When a child is given choices in the learning process it alters the brain chemistry, allowing the neural transmitters to connect more effectively. Help children learn by challenging them with choices!

CONNECTIONS: By connecting the dots in the brain, learning occurs and memory is built. When teaching new material, connect it to something that the students already know. These connections help move the information from the short-term to the long-term memory.

DISCIPLINE: Discipline is very important in the learning process. When discipline is perceived as part of the discipleship process, it can become a positive impetus in the learning experience. The use of fears and threats in discipline will diminish the learning process.

DRAMA: Drama can be a very exciting addition to the learning process. Having children act out their lessons or create dramas, commercials, or other related activities that involve the entire body can be very effective in the classroom.

EMOTIONS: In Chapter 6 we explored the concept of multiple intelligences. There has been much research showing that emotional intelligence is a vital intelligence. Emotions are a distillation of learned wisdom. Children who have a strong emotional intelligence have great people skills and can do much to serve in the kingdom of God. These children are easy to cherish because they are so very lovable. We can challenge them to use their gifts by giving them opportunities to welcome new students and to help with conflict resolution and peace keeping in the classroom. If you have a student with emotional intelligence who may not feel as smart as someone else, you may encourage them by saying, "People are smart in different ways. You are so smart with people and that is a very special intelligence that is hard to teach. People can study harder for tests and do better, but you have God-given smarts in this area." (EQ as apposed to IQ is emotional quota instead of intellectual quota.)

ENVIRONMENT: There is much that we can do to enrich the learning environment. For further information on enriching the learning environment, see Chapter 8.

FEAR: Studies show that when a student is fearful, the learning process is inhibited. Teachers have extraordinary power over children in the classroom. Younger children take every word that the teacher says as absolute truth. With this comes the responsibility to use words that encourage children and not put them down. If a child of any age fears that a teacher might embarrass him in front of his peers by teasing, ridicule, or put-downs, he will experience internal fear and the learning process will be inhibited.

FEEDBACK: Feedback is vital in the learning process. For all of us, we like to know how we are doing. Without some mechanism in place for feedback, we begin to doubt ourselves. Frankly, for many, negative feedback is better than none at all. It is the absence of feedback that eliminates behaviors. While this might be a helpful technique with discipline, it is destructive in the learning process. When we smile and provide words of encouragement, students are energized and empowered to want to do more.

GAMES: Games provide an excellent avenue through which the brain can be challenged. Enhance brain development through challenging learning games.

GIFTEDNESS: I believe strongly that each child is gifted by God for His purpose. When we as educators can find this giftedness, we can cherish and challenge children to be all that they can be.

HELPLESSNESS: When children feel helpless, they sense that they have no control. Helplessness can be a result of a trauma, or it can be a learned behavior. If a child is allowed to use helplessness to prevent him from acquiring new skills or digesting new information, in time it can literally rewire the brain. Learning comes from doing and trying. If a child feigns helplessness to keep from trying, it may be because his earlier attempts were heavily criticized, a parent or caretaker does everything for him, he may be afraid of failure, or he may simply be exhibiting a lazy spirit. In any of these cases, I say to the child: "Have you ever watched a baby trying to learn to walk? Do you know how many times a baby falls before he begins to really walk? When you were a baby, if you gave up every time you fell you would never be able to walk today. It's by trying, sometimes falling, and trying again that we learn."

HEMISPHERICITY: While there is no such a thing as a person being left brained or right brained, there is evidence to show that certain brain functions occur in the left side of the brain such as logical, linear processing, doing one task at a time, and analyzing. Students are considered left brained who like specific assignments, working independently, specific feedback, and competition.

Students are considered more right brained who are more creative, work best relationally, can work on several projects at one time, and like human interest stories to remember facts. As educators we need to provide both kinds of learning experiences in the classroom to facilitate the learning strengths of both. Most of us move back and forth using a combination of each hemisphere's strengths.

INTEGRATION: It is wise to examine curriculum in light of current brain research. Does the curriculum integrate active learning with multisensory learning techniques? Active learning is when we engage the learner in the process. This is best done with multisensory, hands-on teaching. Passive learning is when the teacher lectures and the students listen. While there is a small minority

There is no such thing as being left brained or right brained.

of students who can learn this way, most young children need to be actively involved in the process. Since children learn via their senses, this is the best way to teach.

INTERCONNECTIVITY: This is a similar concept. Think of the brain like a string of Christmas lights. As one lights up, they all do. Likewise when one goes out, they all do. Brain research shows us that when we provide learning opportunities that are multisensory and learner engaged, it causes the parts of the brain to light up and brain connections between isolated pieces of information begin to form.

JOBS: As children come to understand how they learn, it leads them to see what kinds of jobs are better for them. If they are more global and creative, they may not enjoy being an accountant. If they like things to be very analytic, they may not make good artists or musicians. God has a plan for each of our lives and the more we learn about how we learn, the more we come to see that He has wired us for His purpose. This helps us as educators with HEART to shape the hearts of our students.

JOY: When the learning environment is a joyful place, the learning process is facilitated. This does not imply that every aspect of the learning process needs to be fun or silly. It simply means that the basic learning environment is a joyful place, where children feel cherished and challenged. Humor heals. The Scriptures tell us that the joy of the Lord is our strength (Nehemiah 8:10).

KINESTHETIC LEARNING: Kinesthetic learning involves muscle memory. There is much in this book on the value of kinesthetic learning. It is often the area where most teachers feel uncomfortable since it may appear to be out of control. As we study and work with kinesthetic learners, we see many great deeds that can be accomplished by those who must move in order to learn.

KINESTHETICS IN THE LEARNING ENVIRONMENT: Kinesthetics is the study of touch, space, and motion. Research at St. John's University by Dr. Rita Dunn and Dr. Ken Dunn clearly demonstrated that the room arrangement, lighting, degree of kinesthetic learning involved, temperature, and time of day made a significant impact on learning (Dunn & Dunn 1972).

LATERALS: Through forming cross laterals, the brain is able to connect different points of information. This can be done by having the students stand and cross their arms in the air, march by crossing their arms back and forth, and/or pretending to swim. Outdoor activities such as swimming, marching, playing tennis, and roller skating enhance the ability of the brain to make cross lateral connections.

LIGHTING: Lighting is another factor in the learning process that must be examined. Students who feel more comfortable processing information from the left hemisphere of their brains tend to learn more efficiently under bright light. This may include overhead lights, lamps, and windows. Students who are more comfortable functioning from the right side of their brain usually do not learn as well under bright, fluorescent lights. In fact, studies show that bright light may actually fragment the learning process for these students. Try using just a soft lamp or natural lighting.

MOTOR STIMULATIONS: Motor stimulation activates the neural connections in the brain to facilitate learning and long-term memory. For many of us we learn best when we do it ourselves. We build in this muscle memory. For example, with cell phones and programming in the frequently used phone numbers, many of us can no longer remember certain numbers when asked. Before we used programmed numbers and our fingers did the talking, one could put their hand over the phone buttons and the muscle memory in our fingers could retrieve a number. Children in a classroom sometimes move their fingers. I encourage teachers to allow this because if you look more closely you will see that children may be literally typing the words as the teacher says them or doing math on their fingers. This is a positive use of muscle memory. If it facilitates the learning process, why not use it?

MUSIC: While the brain does have two sides, it is not accurate to say that a person is left brained or right brained. The two halves work in conjunction to create a complicated learning network. It is important that we understand what functions are produced on each side while understanding that they work in conjunction with one another. For example: the left hemisphere is more analytic in nature and processes information in a very logical, linear fashion. This is the part of the brain that perceives details first, then patterns, and finally the big picture. The right hemisphere is more global and tends to see the big picture before the details. It tends to be the part of the brain that is more creative. Interestingly, music

> Music is the one activity that utilizes the left and right hemispheres of the brain equally.

is the one activity that utilizes the left and right hemispheres of the brain equally. Therefore, music training is a key component in the learning process. Studies have even shown that classical music enhances brain development. By incorporating music into your classroom you are enhancing the learning environment.

NEGATIVES: Negative ionization is actually what you want in the learning environment! Stuffy classrooms actually have a positive ionization count of 1000. However, a waterfall has a negative ionization of −100,000! Fresh air creates a negative ionization, which has a powerful effect on the learning process. This may seem contrary to what we might think, but indeed it is negative ionization that facilitates the learning process. Make sure the air in your classroom isn't stuffy or stale. Get some fresh air moving and enhance the learning environment!

NOVELTY: New situations simply wake the brain up! Let's plan something completely different and out of the ordinary when our students seem to be growing lethargic.

ODORS: Most of us can be immediately transported back to a place that we recall by the odor. This can be both positive and negative. Brain research provides a lengthy explanation of why this is true. Eric Jensen writes in *Teaching with the Brain in Mind* that "our olfactory memory has minimal erosion and smells go directly to the frontal lobe on the direct expressway to the brain" (1998). Brain research shows that when there is a subtle, good odor in the classroom, it sends the brain a message that this is a positive place to be and learning is enhanced. A word to the wise, wonderful teachers have taken this so to heart that they have used scented candles or the plug-in scents. This is a great idea for most children, but for those who may have an allergic response to the smells, it becomes negative. A soft and subtle smell is best. Beware of strong scents, perfumes, or flowers that are too strong and keep in mind that the plug-in smells for children may be too intense.

OPENNESS: Being open to new ideas is one of the brain's best ways to enhance learning. People who are closed minded and say, "But I have always done it this way," are not being open to change and may inadvertently cause learning to slow down.

PERIPHERY LEARNING: Periphery learning occurs when teachers preview new lessons and provide stimulating learning charts, bulletin boards, and other visuals as part of the learning environment.

PLANTS: Living plants have been shown to have a positive impact on learning environments.

QUESTIONS: Students need to feel comfortable asking questions in order to facilitate their own learning processes. A teacher with HEART will remember to allow time for questions and answers.

QUIET TIMES: These are very necessary components in the learning process. Times of active learning need to be balanced with quiet times in order to maximize long-term memory.

REPITITION: In order for neurons to function properly, they need repetition. Therefore, use multisensory learning techniques in order to build the neuron patterns that make these important learning connections. You could read a Bible verse and then sing it, sign it (with sign language or hand signals), sing and sign it, sign in silence, chant it, and even clap to it. In time your students will know the verse completely.

REST: This is the common denominator that is involved in long-term memory. In order for the brain to function at an optimum level, it requires periods of rest. Provide a variety of learning activities in order to allow children's minds to rest rather than bombard them with lesson material for the entire class time.

SENSORY LEARNING: The senses are the avenues through which learning takes place. When there is sensory stimulation, learning is enhanced. When there is sensory deprivation, learning diminishes. Incorporate activities into your lessons that require your students to use different senses to maximize learning.

SMELLS: Gentle and soft aromas have a very positive effect on the learning environment. Smells conjure up positive memories, which enhances learning. Smells that positively influence learning include lavender, lemon, peppermint, and cinnamon. Smells have a direct expressway to the brain, which is why they are so important in the learning process. They are literally only a synapse away!

TEMPERATURE: Some people learn best when the room is cool, others when the room is warm, and others have no preference. This makes it difficult in any learning environment because there is no way to please everyone. Teachers may take an informal survey of the students in upper elementary and high school to see what the preferences are and from this, set students in different places depending upon where the vents are located.

TIME: Research shows that students learn differently according to the time of day. Research results indicate that older students (high school) actually do better with difficult material after 10:00 A.M. Younger children, on the other hand, do better in the early morning and start winding down as the day progresses.

UNDERSTAND that things take time. As the saying goes, Rome wasn't built in a day! Be patient with yourself as you are trying to incorporate some of these ideas into your teaching. There is a chart at the back of this chapter to help you organize your favorite ideas. Try one a week and by the end of the year you will see that your teaching has dramatically changed. Also, current brain research is developing new ideas all the time. But what keeps your brain alive and well is trying new ideas! So you will enhance your own brain development as well as your students' by incorporating new ideas.

> **Language develops as children interact with adults. Use more active language with your students.**

VIDEOS: Videos, DVDs, tapes, and television do not help children develop language skills. True language development comes from young children interacting with adults. There are four lobes in the brain, and parts of the parietal lobe are not being developed in young children today. The parietal lobe is the top of our upper brain. It is one of the four major areas of the cerebrum and deals with receiving sensory information. It also plays a part in reading, writing, language, and calculation. The other three lobes are the occipital, temporal, and frontal. Encourage teachers to use more active language with their students and less time using videos or tapes.

VISUAL learning is one of the sensory gateways. This can be used to enhance learning by teaching your students how to visualize information in their brain. Color coding can be used to enhance their retrieval process. For example, they can think of the colored note card that they wrote the information down on, or the color highlighter they used on a particular word. As they use these visual cues, they enhance their memories.

WATER: The brain must have water in order to function properly. When the brain is fully hydrated, the learning connections are dramatically facilitated and learning is enhanced. Make sure the children in your class are given rest periods and provide drinks or drink breaks. It is not enough to assume that children are getting these needs met at home before coming to class.

e**X**ERCISE: Exercise is vitally important in the learning process because it produces a hormone that facilitates nerve growth. Exercise also enhances neural connections and elevates the mood of the learner. This important process assists in developing long-term memory for children. Incorporate games and physical activities into your lesson planning to help boost the moods of your students and enhance long-term memory for what you're teaching!

YAWNING is misunderstood in our culture. Most people think that yawning is a sign of sleepiness but actually yawning is a method of self arousal. *The Owner's Manual for the Brain* states, "The yawning response appears to be triggered when dopamine falls below acceptable levels in the brain. The yawn exercises jaw muscles that affect the flow of blood to the brain. A good yawn reoxygenates the brain, leading to increased arousal and alertness" (Howard 1994).

ZOOS are rich in multisensory experiences. A student can see, smell, hear, and sometimes touch the animals. It makes for a great field trip for children. Some churches bring in petting zoos for the children on special Sundays.

Understanding Brain Orientation

Answer the following questions regarding your personal views about the children you teach and how current research on brain orientation applies to your classroom.

1. What is the value of secular research in child development?

2. How does this relate to the understanding that all truth is God's truth?

3. What do you love about children in general?

4. What do you especially enjoy about the age of the children you teach?

5. Has this chapter caused you to consider teaching another age? Why or why not?

6. What do you know of how Jesus feels about children?

7. What are some ways you can apply the attitude of Christ to your teaching ministry to children?

8. As a teacher with HEART, what are some practical ways you can apply child development research to your teaching?

9. List three brain dos and don'ts that you will implement in your classroom (see page 102).

10. What does creating a brain-friendly environment mean to you? How can you go about achieving this? What are three areas of change you want to try for this year?

Brain Based Dos and Don'ts

The following chart is to help you remember what to do and what not to do in your classroom based on how children's brains function.

Because the brain . . .	We do . . .	We don't . . .
functions better with lots of water resulting in enhanced alertness . . .	allow students to have access to water and allow appropriate rest room breaks.	discourage drinking water because of the need for more rest room breaks.
performs many functions simultaneously . . .	present material through a variety of ways in an enriched environment.	teach to only one modality resulting in a dull classroom environment.
needs both focused attention and peripheral perception for an ideal learning environment . . .	provide a learning environment that is positive, offers peripheral learning aids, and encourages the learner.	provide a sterile classroom that is void of encouragement, enrichment, or empowerment via the senses.
is designed to perceive and generate patterns . . .	present information so children can identify patterns and connect them with previous, real-life experiences.	waddle in the wasteland of work sheets.
uses emotions for crucial storage and recall of information . . .	provide an environment that encourages, energizes, and empowers students.	teach as if the feelings of the students are an invalid component to the learning process. ignore the validity of color in the teaching process.
reacts to colors that enhance brain activity . . .	think about the impact of color when planning an activity.	ignore the validity of color in the teaching process.
responds to plants that increase productivity in learning . . .	carefully select plants such as philodendrons, fichus, yellow chrysanthemums,and gerbera daisies to place in the classroom environment.	only put artificial plants in our classroom, even though they do provide needed color and variety. Remember to add live plants also.
does not function solely on the left or right side . . .	provide integrated learning activities.	label our students as being right or left brained.
simultaneously perceives and creates wholes and parts . . .	design learning activities that depict the whole and then break it into parts.	teach only the analytic parts without the context of the whole.
has at least two types of memory: the spatial, which records daily experiences, and rote learning, which deals with skills and facts . . .	teach information and skills based on prior experiences in order to provide frame on which to hang new information to facilitate learning and to promote long-term retention of the information.	overlook rote learning because it does not take into account the learner's personal understanding and retention of the material.
is stimulated by aromas that enhance alertness and memory . . .	provide aromas like peppermint, lemon, cinnamon, and rosemary to stimulate alertness and lavender, orange, and chamomile to regulate stress.	ignore this important point because it seems too feminine.
is affected by lighting in regards to alertness and responsiveness . . .	find ways to provide the best lighting for our students.	rely on the traditional, fluorescent lighting only.
is unique from child to child and its structure is changed by learning . . .	use a wide variety of teaching strategies that include projects, demonstrations, and integrating the information into genuine experiences.	provide information in a boring manner, in only one teaching style, and neglect taking the time to relate it to the personal experience of the learner.

Chapter 8

Cherishing and Challenging Children by Enhancing and Enriching Your Classroom Environment

A Teacher with HEART uses every aspect of the environment to reflect Christ.

Scripture: "Give yourselves fully to the work of the Lord, because you know that your labor in the Lord is not in vain" (1 Corinthians 15:58).

Teaching Objective: To find effective ways to use every aspect of the environment to teach Christ.

The Classroom Environment

Assessing Your Classroom

Try an experiment. Walk around your classroom on your knees and observe your environment closely. You will be amazed. You will see things that you have never seen before, or at the very least, your perspective of your room will change dramatically. This is how your room looks to the children you teach. What can you do to enrich this environment? What can you do to facilitate and maximize the learning process for your students?

Before we begin to look at the environment, let's take a look at the children we teach. We must remember that every child is an individual, uniquely patterned for God's purposes. And every child needs to develop as a balanced individual. If one part develops too rapidly it may be at the expense of another. For example, a child who is skyrocketing intellectually is often paying the price emotionally. Wise teachers will enrich their students' environment to facilitate physical, emotional, mental, and spiritual growth.

Physically Enriching the Environment

• Order: Young children (18 months to 3 years) are in the process of ordering and organizing their environment so they can integrate all of the information coming in via their senses. Providing a place for everything helps children to organize their environment.

You may be saying, "Are you kidding? You haven't seen my students—they don't have an orderly bone!" Try picking out the favorite toys or items of those in your classroom. Put them on a low shelf, with a clearly designated place for each one.

For example:

You may designate the proper place by using a picture (such as from a catalog),

a colored dot or shape on the shelf and the same colored dot or shape on the toy,

or a word label.

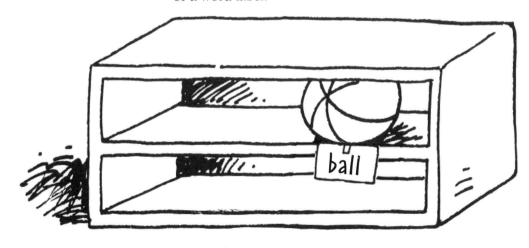

As children learn to match and line up the pictures, geometric shapes, and even words, they are learning more levels of organization. You may add more items to the shelves when the children can handle putting these items away. But be prepared for a delightful surprise. Your children will start putting your things away as well. Be careful, it may be your lesson plans, your important papers, favorite book, or even your car keys!

As children experience order, they will come to want more of it. Believe it or not children have a very strong need for order, especially around ages 2 and 3.

• Categorize: Separate loose items into containers so your children will learn to categorize. Again, label the container, code it, or put a picture on it. If things get out of order, sit down with your children, line up the containers, and reorganize. If you verbalize as you go you will have provided the most wonderful hands-on lesson in organizing. You will reap rich dividends in laying the foundation for teaching children to be organized learners.

A word to the wise—start simple.

Begin with a few mainline toys such as:	Graduate to containers for items such as:
• Stackable rings	• Crayons
• Pegboard	• Blocks
• Stacking tower	• Trucks/cars
• Simple four-piece puzzles	• Figurine dolls

Do not overwhelm or complicate the situation by providing too many items or too many containers. Slowly add items as your children demonstrate that they can effectively organize and care for them.

I suggest that you not buy toy boxes. They teach nothing. A child simply learns to pull out, play, and throw the toys back in. Instead, purchase low shelves and put them in different areas of your room. This communicates to the children; "You are a very special and integral part of our class. You belong here." You can purchase inexpensive stackable shelves that can be placed strategically around your room.

• Color: We all respond to color, whether or not we are aware of it. Bright red stimulates and may even cause overstimulation. Blue soothes and has a calming influence. Green and light peach have been used by hospitals because of their healing effect. Yellow is a mentally stimulating color.

Research shows that the primary colors are better for babies because they are easier to discriminate. Many teachers, care centers, and schools have responded accordingly. Yet so many of us still prefer the pastel colors for babies. Why? Perhaps because the pastel colors are so soothing to us as adults.

Color is a fun concept to play with. Play color games with your students. "I wonder what an elephant would look like red." Color different colors in a coloring book instead of just the traditional and expected color choices. Get a prism and look at different colors. Paint rainbows in a different order. Let your students' color creativity abound!

There is another way to physically enrich your classroom environment using color. If you have a number of children who display choleric or dynamic personalities, you may want to calm them down with a quiet blue or green room. Red, yellow, and orange may be too stimulating. Your quiet, withdrawn, and perhaps moody melancholy and analytic children may do well with the cheery stimulus of soft yellow. Red and orange may be too irritating to them, and blue and green may pull them deeper into themselves.

Emotionally Enriching the Environment

Provide a warm, loving, nurturing environment. Remember to touch, love, and affirm children. Praise the children's attempts to learn and master their environment. Appreciate the uniqueness of the children you teach. Strengthen your faith by trusting that God made children in need of training and guidance, but recognize that their unique designs came from God.

Children are like sponges. They absorb what is around them physically as well as emotionally. As you examine what you have placed in their environment, reflect on what messages you are sending. What do you want them soak up? To absorb? To mirror back?

If you talk too loudly, how can you expect them to be quiet? If you are easily upset or rattled, how can you expect them to be gentle and loving? If you neglect to verbally affirm their efforts, how can you expect them to reflect back a positive self-image?

Children are born mimics. It is often easy to spot behaviors that children have learned from their parents. For example, men who are gruff in expressing their feelings often influence little boys to reflect the same body language and mannerisms. One day a friend

> **God made children in need of training and guidance.**

lamented that her children didn't seem to show any respect for her. When I saw the way her husband treated her in front of the child, I realized that until her husband changed and modeled a respectful attitude, the child would think that it was OK to treat his mother with little respect. Remember, patterns of emotional response are generally formed by the time a child is 5 years old and it takes many years and much hard work to change these patterns.

Mentally Enriching the Environment

We need to realize two very important and distinctive differences in the way that children and adults perceive work and play. Adults often work for a living and play to relax. For children, work is play and play is work. A paradox? Let's explore this concept.

Children are close observers of the adult world. They imitate what they see. As they pretend to dress up, cook dinner, hammer nails, and mow the lawn, they are very happy. They do not perceive this work as a tiring process.

The work of children differs profoundly from that of adults in its purpose, procedure, and production. The work of adults is usually to produce something external in the world, whereas the work of children is intended to produce internal results. The purpose of the work of children is to create the skills necessary to build the adults they are to be.

It is wise to create an environment filled with child-size work as seen from the adult world. For example, provide orderly ways for children to learn how to properly organize materials, complete a task and put items away, clean up a center, keep their area neat, or organize their work

We may categorize this as work and think that children need to go to their toys to play. However, for children who function best when they can experience their environment via all of the senses, work and play are synonymous, especially when they are allowed to explore and discover on their own.

Likewise, the very process of playing is part of the work of childhood that constructs the inner person. Just as children imitate the work that they see adults do, they also play back real-life situations, both happy and sad. As they play out these experiences, they slowly integrate reality into their understanding.

To illustrate this point, let's take a child who has just had a very painful and unexpected shot at the doctor's office. The well-meaning adult in her life, whom she trusts completely, has said, "This is good for you. But it will sting for a minute."

> **For children, work is play and play is work. They imitate what they see.**

Within this communication are many vague words that are meaningless to a child with her current level of understanding. *Sting? Minute? Too vague. Good? Oh, good, that's a nice word.* She hears a semi-comforting tone in the adult's voice, but she feels stress. Lots of confusing signals. Then, whammo! Here comes the shot. Ouch! It hurts like crazy. *This is for my good—are you kidding?* She looks at the adult and mistrust may set in. Now what?

A child needs to integrate this painful, confusing experience into her own level of understanding. How can she do this most effectively? By playing it back into her reality. Observe her. She may pretend to be the doctor or nurse and give her stuffed animal or baby doll a shot. She verbalizes those silly nonsense words and may even add a few of her own. She integrates the pain and confusion into her own life experience, and in doing so, reduces the pain. She takes a situation in which she had no control, puts herself in the driver's seat, and recreates the scene. Each time she does this, the stress level is reduced. Play heals.

Allow opportunities for creative, imaginative play. Let children talk to themselves, to imaginary friends, and with their toys. Play is healing. Children will often say more to a puppet, animal, or doll than they will to an adult. Don't hinder this creative play for children. It is as constructive as work is.

One way to enrich the mental environment is with books. I cannot state strongly enough the profound importance of reading to your students. Reading is rewarding for many reasons. It allows children to hear the patterning of language even before they can understand it or speak it—reading to them strengthens their ability to master language skills.

Reading to children also teaches them to create pictures in their minds. It helps them to see the relationship between the written word and images, and strengthens their own ability to read.

We are not reading to children so they will learn to read early. Reading should be done to enrich, encourage, involve, and develop our students' language skills.

Provide a wide variety of intellectually stimulating activities. By this I mean provide items that challenge children's minds but are still age appropriate. I do not mean to imply that you need to provide every gimmicky toy on the market that guarantees to raise a child's IQ. We do not want to create an academic pressure cooker for our students. Instead, seek to provide a variety of life-based experiences to help in discovering how God created these unique people. As we provide music, books, puzzles, and stimulating

> Allow opportunities for imaginative play. Children will often say more to a puppet, animal, or doll than to an adult.

activities, we learn how God gifted the children we teach. A word to the wise—while you seek to challenge your students to be the most they can be, be careful not to rush them. You do not want to over stimulate or over educate them.

Dr. David Elkind, in his books *The Hurried Child* (1981) and *All Dressed Up with No Place to Go* (1997), clearly articulates the dangers of giving too much to children too soon. That is why a balance of work and play is so essential. Enriching the environment mentally does not imply that we do every intellectual activity to produce brighter and better children. It means that we provide a stimulating environment with a wide variety of options that encourage children to experience and interact with all their senses, thus challenging them.

Spiritually Enriching the Environment

Provide areas where children can be quiet, reflective, and contemplative. For example, on a low shelf place a Bible (or a picture Bible for young children) and something of beauty from God's world. Children will spontaneously go and sit there quietly. It seems to feed and nourish their souls with God's peace.

Have posters or pictures that show children being loving, kind, and gentle. Be sure that they are at a child's eye level.

If your students can read, place Bible verses around the room that will help them deal with character-trait qualities. For example: "A gentle answer turns away wrath, but a harsh word stirs up anger" (Proverbs 15:1).

When you share these items with your students, do so in a quiet voice. As you communicate love and reverence for our Lord and His world, children will begin to model this after you.

Learning Modalities and the Environment

We can ease the stress load for children by enriching their environment in a way that suits their learning modality. After reading Chapter 4 you have probably identified many of your students as visual, auditory, tactile, or kinesthetic learners. Armed with that information, you can do much to enrich their environment in a way that best meets their needs.

God created us to be cocreators, and in utilizing this creative energy we find ourselves most content. Do more creative things with your students. Paint, work with clay, read books, go on field trips, or go exploring! In the process you will discover so many more opportunities to share God's Word with your students.

Ease a child's stress by enriching their environment in a way that maximizes their comfort zone.

Creating Creative Learning Environments

Making your learning environments creative is critical. Your classrooms or large assembly areas may be the first attraction your children experience. Children should be attracted by what they see and experience in your facilities. If your environments attract them, they may mentally stick around for deeper things. If your environments are cold and sterile, the children may mentally leave before you even begin your lesson.

Creative Doorways

If you think about it, the doorway is the first thing the parents or children actually see as they approach your room (unless you are standing outside greeting them). There are things you can do to the doorway that make it a tool of your lesson as well. You can decorate it with some lesson-related decoration. You can build a puppet stage in the doorway and perform a short introductory show either before the children enter the room, or right after they come in. You can hang things from the doorway so the children have to walk in through something that introduces the lesson topic. You can also make a doorway cut-out that the children walk through. Think of your doorway as the entrance to the learning environment!

Creative Walls

When the parents or children first see the room, they should be attracted to your lesson topic. A good teacher makes the walls a part of the lesson. Fight the temptation to just stick a picture from your curriculum on the wall! That doesn't interest anyone! You don't have to produce a piece of art each week, just ask God to help you create a word, a statement, or something that intrigues the children or makes them ask, "What's that for?" as they walk in. For instance, if your lesson topic is about controlling your anger, you might write the question "Is it ever right to fight?" on the board. As the parents or children see that question, they will begin to think about the answer, or even talk about the question among themselves. You've attracted them to the lesson topic without even saying a thing! You can also put up a picture or series of pictures that pertain to the topic without any explanation. Then ask the children to figure out what your lesson topic is for the day. Consider the use of the bulletin boards, white (chalk) boards, windows, upper wall cabinets, or plain wall space.

Creative Floors

Floors are perhaps the most under-appreciated surface in your room. Floors can be fun. You can draw on them with masking tape, tape messages on them, or transform them into a game board. You can also place unusual, lesson-related objects on the floor. You can create a "lesson treasure trail" that the children follow and experience lesson centers along the way. You can also rearrange, or remove, the furniture to suit your lesson topic.

The bottom line of transforming your room into a creative learning environment is to think outside the box of your own habits or preconceptions. If you get an idea and you react with a thought of, "That can't be done," I would encourage you to try it. It is usually those "can't be done" ideas that the children will never forget!

Excerpt from *Growing a Healthy Children's Ministry* by Steve Alley. Standard Publishing, 2002.

Learning Modalitites and the Environment

Use the following chart to identify ways you can enrich your classroom environment to engage students with various learning modalities.

	Visual	Auditory	Tactile/Kinesthetic
Physically	Needs to SEE lots of things in the physical environment.	Needs to HEAR things in the physical environment.	Needs to TOUCH things in the physical environment.
	Needs to have an orderly physical environment.	Needs to be able to speak frequently.	Needs to be able to move in the physical environment.
	Make a chart for goals or behavior modification where a child can see his progress with ✓, ★ or sticker.	Needs to feel comfortable with the communication process.	Needs lots of child-developmentally appropriate things to manipulate and learn with.
	Paint the room or add colors that have a positive affect on your students.		
Emotionally	Remember, these learners are acute observers of visual clues such as facial expressions and body language. Be expressive, but be sure you are communicating the message you want to communicate.	Praise verbally: "I'm so happy with how you cleaned up your work!" "I'm so blessed to have you in my classroom."	Hug, touch, pat, etc. to show love and warmth.
	Show facial expressions that suggest love, appreciation, and approval.	Articulate your feelings so the student learns the language of emotionally relating to others.	Expect that this child will show his feelings by touching.
	Display posters that demonstrate character traits that you are trying to teach, such as sharing, loving, and serving.	Ignore stuttering! It is a stage that will pass in most cases if a child is loved and encouraged through it. Please don't say, "Don't stutter."	Encourage appropriate ways to show feelings by touching.
			Be emotionally supportive and accepting of this child's extra needs to move and touch.
Mentally	Providing lots of mentally stimulating things for the students to look at on an age-appropriate level. Things on the wall, on the child's eye level should include: *Preschool:* Colors, Shapes, Letters, Numbers, Animals. *Elementary:* Maps, Cursive alphabet (grade 2), Manuscript alphabet (K-1st) with upper and lower case and items that start with that sound. Ex: Aa	Provide a variety of things for preschool children to listen to as well as sing and/or talk along with, *Night-time:* Lullabies, Story tapes/CDs, Quiet song tapes/CDs *Fun and Movement:* Hap Palmer, Ella Jenkins, Donut Man, Mary Rice Hopkins. *Teaching:* Hap Palmer, Visit a teacher supply store and get acquainted with the interesting tapes available.	Provide age-appropriate things for each child to touch and manipulate. For example: *Preschool:* Puzzles of letters or numbers IF the child shows an interest, Let children trace letters or numbers so they can touch, see, and hear you say the sound simultaneously. *Elementary:* Let the child write letters in a tray of sand. Let the child write letters in finger-paint. Let the child spell words in frosting or pudding and then lick his fingers!

Learning Modalitites and the Environment (Continued)

	Visual	**Auditory**	**Tactile/Kinesthetic**
Mentally (continued)	Keep lots of age-appropriate books, games, and toys readily available.	Play verbal games where the child listens, repeats, or responds on his own.	Provide an environment where the child feels free to move, touch, and explore instead of being told, "Don't touch," "Sit still," or "No!"
	Arrange a creative corner with lots of open-ended items for the child to see, pretend, imagine and create with.	Build in listening as well as talking skills.	
	Check out paintings from the library and hang them up for 2 weeks to expose your students to the arts. Point out things for them to see—help them to see art.	Arrange a creative corner where children can make believe, play, and pretend. Allow them to talk to themselves as they play.	
Spiritually	Put up pictures for preschoolers and verses (with or without pictures) that reflect godly attitudes or lessons you are teaching. For example, when you are teaching the 23rd Psalm, put up a gentle picture of a shepherd and a lamb for a preschooler. For the elementary-age child, put up part or all of the 23rd Psalm printed so he can read it.	Play tapes of Bible stories and songs.	Let children manipulate Bible learning materials such as Noah's Ark, items in God's creation, Bible puzzles, Bible maps, etc.
	Read the Bible and/or Bible-related books, daily!	Read to your students from Bible or Bible-related books.	Let children make things from clay to represent different Bible verses.
	Provide time daily for children to "read" and look at books. Encourage appropriate and frequent use of books.	Allow children to "read" books back to you.	Dramatize Bible lessons.
		Say and sing Scripture verses.	

The Environment and Brain Orientation

A teacher with HEART knows the importance of enriching the learning environment to facilitate learning. Neuroscientists are still learning about all the brain can do. Brain cells are formed between the fourth and seventh months of gestation and a newborn has five trillion connections in the brain. The human brain is literally the most responsive organ we have. Child development teaches us that the first 48 months of life are the most critical. The implications of this for us as teachers with HEART are extremely important.

When we enrich the environment of the children we teach, we can do much to facilitate the learning process. We can enrich with colors, sounds, soft light, and a beautiful multisensory environment. The brain connections do best with a rich landscape of a well thought-out sensory environment.

When we expose a child to enhanced learning, we see that his brain changes. Further changes occur when a child's brain experiences something firsthand. Again, in an environment that is filled with hands-on, multisensory learning, a child's brain connections increase dramatically. Thus we equip the learner by encouraging, empowering, and energizing them in the learning process. For each of us, when we experience success, we learn faster. What is the secret to getting smarter? Brain connections! The more that we increase the synaptic connections between brain cells, the smarter we get.

The implications for teaching children are vitally important. The more that we expose them to the Word of God, and help to make it come alive with firsthand experiences in a loving and positive environment, we help move these learning experiences into a child's long-term memory. Brain research shows that it is the number of direct experiences that determine which brain synapses are kept and which are discarded. Let us be thinking of ways to help children experience the Word of God more directly.

Examining the Environment

As we look at the environment, we must look at it through the learning process. First there must be a stimulus for the brain to begin its work. Then this stimulus is stored and becomes the potential for memory. Multisensory experiences enhance this process. If we could view this process in the form of a brain scan, we would see that when a new task is initiated the brain lights up, and the light diminishes when the task is completed. Again, the best way to move a short-term memory to a long-term positive memory is through creating a positive learning environment.

> How often a child directly experiences the lesson material affects whether or not the brain retains or discards that information.

> **Encouraging words are vital in order to move information from short-term to long-term memory.**

Engage with episodic memory. This simply means that learning and memory are two sides of a coin. In a sense it is a house of mirrors that is always changing. Episodic memory is simply moving learning to long-term potentiation, or LTP. Brain research tells us that this is best facilitated in a positive learning environment. The power of encouraging words is vital in order to move information from short-term to long-term memory.

Energy is needed for brain boosters. This involves eating healthy food, drinking lots of water, which increases the brain connections, providing good air to breathe, and minimizing the chemicals in the environment. Included in this is providing time for movement! Children need to move and movement provides necessary brain boosters. Exercise is one of the best brain boosters of all!

Exercise is critical to proper brain development. In this complex culture we live in, children do not run and play for long periods of time. We rush them from one activity to another in a frantic pace. I believe the seeming rise in differences among children as to how they learn is due in great part to a lack of exercise, too much time with video games and a lack of quiet time. I am tremendously excited about a group that works with children to help them find the natural, God-given rhythm within their bodies through a non-evasive technique using a metronome and the child's involvement. It is exciting to see children go through this program, begin to calm down, and focus, the way God created them to be. (For more information, you may look up www.gotofocus.com.)

Endangered Minds: Why Our Children Can't Think (1990): Excellent documentation about the dangers of television, and video games that keep our children from having direct communication and interaction with adults can be found in this book by Jane Healy, Ph.D. As educators we need to enhance the environment with real-life experiences, active learning, and lots of communication, or we will be raising a generation of children with endangered minds.

Children need close, connected interactions with adults in order to develop good people skills. As Christian educators, this is one of our missions. We must seek to provide warm, loving, emotionally enriching, mentally stimulating, and spiritually challenging environments to anchor our students to Jesus Christ.

Your Classroom Environment

Evaluate Your Classroom

Answer the following questions for a closer look at how you can enhance your classroom environment.

1. Walk around on your knees and look at your classroom from a child's viewpoint. Is your room functional for children? (For example, does it have shelves and coat hooks they can reach.)

2. Is the room appealing to children? (Are there some pictures and furniture items at their eye level?)

3. Is it inviting of their presence?

4. Can you see areas where you have enriched the classroom environment to challenge your students? Give examples of appropriate active learning ideas for each area.

Physically?

Emotionally?

Mentally?

Spiritually?

5. Are you allowing time for children to create the people that they are to be as adults? Remember, children create and construct through play. Are you cherishing and challenging each child through providing an enriched environment?

6. For young children, how does work become play and play become work? Why are work and play one in the minds of young children?

Chapter 9

Cherishing and Challenging Children Through Appropriate Classroom Discipline

A Teacher with HEART understands that discipline is an essential element to becoming an effective teacher.

Scripture: "Our fathers disciplined us for a little while as they thought best; but God disciplines us for our good, that we may share in his holiness. No discipline seems pleasant at the time, but painful. Later on, however, it produces a harvest of righteousness and peace for those who have been trained by it" (Hebrews 12:10, 11).

Teaching Objective: To find practical ways of becoming more effective at classroom discipline.

Children respond to the teacher's disposition.

You have just completed a teacher-training course on discipline. You feel confident that you can handle the many challenges set before you. But it's one of those days and the students have pushed all of your buttons. You've been trying out all of the new techniques you have learned, but your frustration level is speaking volumes, and thus, the techniques are not working. You finally lose it big time and in walks the person who led your teacher training. You want to cry . . . or die.

Children are very sensitive to their surroundings, especially to any shift in a teacher's disposition. They often respond with agitation when they perceive frustration from their teacher. They tune in to your wishes easily and have a tendency to react to what they sense in the environment. So it seems that when we want them to behave their very best, they feel our stress, and often the result is an exhibition of their worst behavior. We react to their behavior, they react to our frustration, and the cycle perpetuates.

Do Understand That It Is All About Relationships

First and foremost, how we discipline is directly related to our relationship with the Lord Jesus Christ. As a teacher with HEART, understand that Jesus must be the focus of your heart, and that your thoughts, words and deeds are all filtered through the grid of your relationship with Him. Secondly, discipline is a reflection of your relationship with your students. When they know you love them, and when you take the time to get to know them, discipline issues begin to get easier. Take some time each week to simply get to know your students. Here are a few suggestions to get you started:

NAME CHAIN: Take time to get to know each other's names and something about each other. Have each child say her name and one thing about herself. Do this every week for the first month until you have all gotten to know each other.

BINGO: Each student makes up a bingo card (from the form you provide) in the following way:

"Put your name in the middle."

"Put your favorite color in a box."

"Put your favorite song in a box."

"Put your favorite number in a box."

Continue until all of the boxes are filled. Then, play Bingo and see how many students selected the same color, number, song, etc. (This game is intended for older students.)

CARD GAME: This game follows the same concept as Bingo. Each child has a card with titles such as My Favorite Food, My

Favorite Song, and My Favorite Book written on them. Students interview each other until their cards are filled with responses to these topics, and then share the responses they received with the entire class.

GUESS WHO: Pair this game with the Card Game. Read the cards of favorites to the class and allow children to try to determine who gave each response.

Depend on the Holy Spirit

Children seem to test us continually and are able to quickly push us to our limits. Instead of responding with bursts of frustration, depend on the power of the Holy Spirit and pray for His guidance, so that you do not react in the flesh, but respond in the power of the Holy Spirit. If you take a deep breath, walk slowly to the child, gently cup his face in you hands, look him straight in the eye, and state your desire with a firm but loving voice, he can hear you far better than if you were to yell or to engage in a power struggle.

When you move slowly and quietly and consistently and earnestly pray for the Lord to take control of your responses, you are able to handle discipline far more effectively. It's the Christian version of counting to 10. It slows down human reactions and gives the Holy Spirit a chance to work. Again, children learn more from the essence of who you are, than from what you say. Respond in the power of the Holy Spirit instead of reacting in the flesh.

Do Remember the Power of Prayer

A teacher's character and conduct are contagious when in the presence of children. However, children are not only sensitive to changes in mood but also even to barometric pressure changes! To explain this a little better, let's put two potentially volatile situations together. It's an important day at Sunday school or day school. You are putting on a special program, which you have been working on for some time. You woke up with a bad headache. The children in your class are excited because of the program and hyper because a big storm is rolling into town. Of course, this would also be the day for a traffic accident to cause you to arrive late. Now you're tense, in pain, late, and not feeling on top of things. The children's noise and antics are about to push you over the edge. What's a teacher to do? Here's a suggestion that's easy to remember—P.R.A.Y.:

> **Children learn more from the essence of who you are than from what you say.**

P Pause and Pray

R Remember, this too shall pass—and remember to see the humor; it will change your perception.

A Allow yourself to be used by God, while remembering that in your weakness, He is glorified.

Y Yield yourself as an empty vessel and see what God will do!

Determine to Be Diligent Spiritually

Being diligent involves humbly seeking ways to enhance your discipline techniques and persevering in those things you already know, even when they are emotionally draining or time consuming. The Bible says, "Whoever loves discipline loves knowledge" (Proverbs 12:1). Because the Bible is the greatest source of knowledge, we must study the Word of God daily. It is also wise to read books on the topics of teaching and discipline. Of course, we should be on our knees often, asking God for help in teaching the students He has entrusted to us. Be diligent in your preparations to handle situations requiring discipline. It's better to be over prepared and to have a backup plan in place.

Diligent in the Practical Ways

Be diligent with your practical planning as well. Be sure to have the items in place that you will need in order to implement your plans in a productive manner. It's frustrating when you realize you don't have dry-erase markers, glue sticks, and resources to make your teaching flow more efficiently. Planning ahead can often avert a disaster. It's a wise investment of time.

Planning ahead can often avert a disaster!

Define Your Expectations

As our students grow, so will our expectations for them. However, we must be careful that these expectations grow slowly and are consistent with each child's particular strengths and weaknesses. At different ages children require different preparations for discipline. For example: one of the rhythms of early childhood is that in the even years, starting at age 2, children are more aggressive; and in the odd years, starting at age 3, they are more reflective. Let's look at each age individually:

1-year-olds: These children are in the dart 'n dash stage. You cannot expect them to sit for any amount of time. They love to do the opposite of what you say. They are not so much rebelling as playing a game of what will happen if I do this? You must be willing to chase the child at times and remind them often, but be realistic in what they can actually achieve in terms of discipline.

2-year-olds: These children are actually quite obedient. I do not agree with the expression "the terrible 2s". Usually, a 2-year-old is upset only if his routine is changed, or if he is expected to do more than a 2-year-old can realistically do. Two-year-olds imitate and can be easily trained by an adult modeling appropriate behavior. They love to play games, and almost anything can be made into a game, such as picking up crayons, cleaning up, washing their hands, and walking in a line.

3-year-olds: These children are more introverted and clingy. They may whine and need a little more coaxing. However, they understand most verbal instructions, need and enjoy adult approval, and can be encouraged into proper behavior.

4-year-olds: Now is the time you may experience major discipline challenges. Four-year-olds seem out of bounds. They laugh too hard, cry too hard, play too hard—everything is extreme. This is the age that tries teachers most. At this age it is necessary to carefully and consistently define the rules, set limits, and then take appropriate measures of action when children need to be disciplined. We must also be willing to love and accept children through their extreme ups and downs. On a side note, almost all 4 year olds test as auditory learners. You have probably noticed that they talk whether or not anyone is in the room. Once you realize that this is how they learn you can extend your patience with children at this age.

5-year-olds: They are sweet and compliant and very eager to please adults. Enjoy it, for the 6s are coming! I think God gives us the grace period of age 5 neatly tucked between the 4s and the 6s!

6-year-olds: They are more aggressive and need opportunities to stretch their independence muscles. This is a time to offer some positive choices. For example, "Would you like to build with blocks or create with clay?"

7-year-olds: This is an important time in a child's development process. Children at this age are moving from being concrete learners to learners who can understand more abstract concepts. They are more self-reflective at this age and need love, support, and consistent discipline.

Decide Your System of Cause and Effect

One of the most effective ways for any of us to learn is by reaping the consequences of our own actions. The expression "no pain, no gain" says it well. Thus it is very helpful for anyone working with children to sit down and decide what their system of cause and effect will be. Although it is impossible to anticipate every situation, we can still make a list of general causes and effects. For example:

Cause:	Effect:
• If the child talks back . . .	• She loses a special privilege for that day.
• If the child is caught hitting or fighting . . .	• He must apologize to the person and do something loving with his hands for that person.
• If a child is deliberately disobedient . . .	• Talk with a parent and set up a proactive plan for the appropriate consequence.

One thing that I have found helpful when I am trying to train in a new behavior is to have a marble jar for each classroom. If the students do something spontaneously kind, respectful, or godly, they get a new marble for their jar. Likewise, if they obey right away, displaying a good attitude and positive manners, a marble is added. However, if they do not answer with respect, say something unkind to another student, or take their sweet time with getting around to obeying, they lose a marble. When the class reaches a predetermined number of marbles, they receive a reward.

The obvious negative component in this is that the compliant students always obey, while other students rarely obey—causing the entire class to be penalized. However, a positive factor is that it trains students to put into practice a healthy level of peer monitoring.

The marble jar is not something you should have in place all the time, but it can be used as an effective transition activity when some negative habits are creeping into the classroom. As new positive habits are built, you can wean your students off of this system. Again, Christlike behavior is the goal. However, sometimes something tangible is needed in order to foster improved behavior.

Determine Appropriate Consequences

In order for children to best be trained through discipline, the consequence must be related to the deed as much as possible. Here are a few guidelines to help you in reflecting upon the importance of this in terms of making significant changes in the behavior of children:

- The consequence helps the child to see that her choice determined what happened. This brings accountability into the picture.
- The consequence must maintain the dignity of the child.
- The consequence must be logically connected to the action and occur right away so that the child can see the relationship between the two.
- The teacher must respond only to the current deed, not bringing in a long list of past inappropriate behaviors. Please don't use statements like, "You always . . ." or "You never. . . ."
- Follow through in a consistent manner—exclude emotional drama.

Define Your Basic System

Teachers, ask yourselves, "What are the basic rules for my classroom going to be?" This is a critically important question. Each person comes into teaching with certain expectations and desires for discipline. Pray about what you need for your classroom, define it, write it down, and then communicate your system to the children you teach.

The following three simple rules work for all students, ages 2–18. (With the young students you will need to repeat these guidelines every week.)

1. When you want to talk, you may raise your hand and wait to be called upon. When someone else is talking, you may be quiet.
2. Keep your hands and feet to yourself, unless you have permission to do otherwise.

In order for discipline to be effective, the consequence must be related to the deed as much as possible.

3. Use your words to encourage one another and not to hurt.

State your behavior guidelines in a positive way. Too often teachers spend too much time telling children what they don't want them to do and forget to tell them what they do want them to do. When you state things in a positive way, your voice inflection, and facial expressions are more positive as well, and your students are less inclined to tune you out.

Discuss Your System

After your system is defined, discuss it with the class. Dialogue with them about how they feel about the rules. If your students are older, you may even allow them to be part of the decision-making process. The important thing is to keep the lines of communication open with children as to how the discipline system operates.

You may be saying, "I have a strong-willed student who takes great pleasure in destroying whatever system I set up. The more he knows, the more he tries to outsmart the system." I suggest that you throw the ball back in his court. Say, "John, if you were the teacher, what would you do in this situation?" (Remember, this is the personality who always wants to be in charge.) If the student comes up with a strict and appropriate consequence for his action, say, "This is a great idea, John. You have really made a wise decision. I think we will do just that." Now, if he comes up with a silly, completely inappropriate consequence, you can verbalize, "John, I really think you could come up with a better idea. I guess you're not ready to be in charge of these things yet. We'll try you again later." Believe me; he will work harder the next time. Don't try to break the spirit of these strong-willed children. Instead, learn to channel their strength into more appropriate behavior.

Do Try New Systems

Each teacher has to find a discipline system that works, and be willing to try new ones as well. Here are a few that are helpful:

Find ways to get your student's attention without raising your voice. *The Discipline Guide for Children's Ministry* (Capehart, West, and West 1997) has a lot of practical tips for doing this. My favorites include using: a silly song that is age appropriate (such as "Eyes on me by the time I count to three!") or a bell with a nice soothing melodic quality in which the vibrations go out and can be heard for at least 15 seconds. The bell signals the children to freeze and turn their eyes to you. After you have said what you've needed to say, they may "defrost."

Make a sound meter for your classroom out of poster board. It can be done with age appropriate words or pictures. Turn the arrow to what you want so that the students can see what level is desired instead of needing verbally to remind them:

For older students you could have a class meeting. Discuss the issues and collectively come up with appropriate consequences for inappropriate actions in the classroom. This gives older students ownership of the issues, and peer monitoring will be a great help to you.

A Three-Step Process of Discipline:
- Step One: The first time the student violates the rule, walk slowly to the child and quietly tell him the rule. In other words, assume he caught the prevalent childhood disease of rule amnesia.
- Step Two: The second time the student violates the rule, walk slowly to the student and ask him to tell you what the rule is.
- Step Three: The third time the student violates the rule, walk slowly to the student and enforce an immediate consequence related to the deed.

Remember the following key pointers to help you be successful in your classroom discipline:
- Always walk slowly to the student and keep your eyes on her. There is power in the eyes. As teachers we can talk less and use our eyes more.
- Always stair step your voice down. Ladies, when we are upset, our voices go up. We must train them to go down or children do not take us seriously. As you state what you want the child to do, nod your head up and down and smile. As you state what you do not want them to do, nod your head no. This gives them both verbal and visual cues.
- Ask the child, "Do you understand me?" Wait for a polite response, and if you don't get it, say, "Excuse me?" This is important, as this is your close.
- After the child has responded to you, ask the child to apologize to the other child(ren). Yes, it is true. The child may not be truly repentant. If you wait until he is repentant, he may be 30 years old and that is a long time to wait. I believe in training in the habit of apologizing and trusting the Lord to change the heart and bring about true repentance.

Don't ever turn your back on a child you have just disciplined. Even the sweetest of them may stick out their tongue while your back is turned, and you have just set yourself up for round two. Walk slowly backwards and keep your eyes on the child at all times.
- Act detached. Let me clarify what I mean by detached. You are not detached from the child but rather from the deed. It means that you don't get emotionally engaged in the junk. You may be churning internally, but you play the part of not being upset. Use a more objective tone of voice with the student. Don't allow the student to argue or negotiate with you at this time. You may have to pretend that you are trying

Detach yourself from the deed, not the child. As you detach yourself you are better able to communicate calmly what you expect.

to win an Academy Award in how you present yourself. As you begin to act that way, you may be surprised that you start to feel that way. When you are not acting exasperated and are calmly communicating what you expect, you have a more powerful presence. The students know that you mean business. Remember, in your portrayal of detachment, you are never detached from the child. You will always love your students; you just won't like everything they do.

Pray, as you are walking toward and away from the child, for God to give you the right words.

Do Play Games to Remember the Rules

It is wise to repeat the class rules, or guidelines, on a regular basis. If it is in a Sunday school or Wednesday night environment, it is even more important since the class may have new students. Try stating them in different ways to make it more fun, such as:

- Puppet Plays: Have the puppets tell the rules.
- Rule Unscramble: Scramble up the words and let the students figure them out.
- Picture Signals: What rule is this following or breaking?
- Find the Rules: Hide them around the classroom.
- Wheel of Fortune: Play a game similar to Wheel of Fortune with the letters of the rule turned backwards on the white board. Use a spinner from another game.

Direct Your Attention

Does the following story sound familiar? You have to get your students to another location in 20 minutes and you still need to get the classroom in order. Suddenly Sarah falls down, Adam knocks something over, or Jason starts to whine. What's a teacher to do? As mentioned earlier, children are very sensitive to the teacher's mood. When you are under the most pressure and need the children to behave the best, they often deliver their worst behavior.

The best way to handle such situations is to simply stop and give your students your focused attention. If you ignore your students, yell, or isolate them, the problems crescendo and both parties lose. If they are young, simply holding them will work wonders. Look into their eyes and show them that you are truly focused on them.

The obvious exception to this principle of discipline is if a child has deliberately done something to hurt another child or has intentionally disobeyed you. You have every right to isolate the child in this case. Directing your attention is a practice intended especially for young children who cannot understand why you are so preoccupied.

Remember that acting up is often a child's way of getting the adult attention they so yearn for. If you can provide this attention consistently, your children won't have to go to such lengths to achieve it.

Deal with Details

An old adage states: "Take care of the pennies, and the dollars will take care of themselves." We can apply the same principle to dealing with children. Deal with the details and the big things are often taken care of as well. For example, if we allow our students to talk out without raising their hands, the classroom can quickly become loud and chaotic. Focus on reminding children to wait for their turn to talk, and the overall noise level of the classroom environment will take care of itself.

Another old adage states: "An ounce of prevention is worth a pound of cure." In terms of discipline, this is certainly true. A helpful way to get a handle on this idea is to think through when most of your discipline problems occur. Perhaps it is during transition times. Carefully observe your students at this time for several days. Then make a list of what could be done to make it easier for the children to handle a particular situation. For example:

- Have an action song or game to play if you have to wait for someone such as a special teacher to come to the classroom.

Your students are not out to get you! They're just driven by incessant curiosity.

- Use the time constructively to practice reciting memory verses, quiz using Bible facts, or ask lesson review questions.
- Have clearly defined procedures, such as how to walk in a line. Remind children to place their hands behind their backs and not to talk. For younger children, it may be helpful for them to pretend they have a bubble in their mouths. The children take a breath and form a big pretend bubble in their mouths. It is fun, they love it, and it gives them something to focus on and keeps them from talking.

Direct and Redirect Their Abundant Energy

Children, especially young children, are so incredibly energetic and multisensory. They are fascinated by everything and driven by an incessant curiosity. Some days it may seem that they are out to get you, but they really are just interested in everything. They learn by doing and touching.

As an adult caring for young children, you must often direct or redirect them into purposeful activities. It is also wise to childproof the area as much as possible. This action is far better for the child's self-esteem than reprimanding, continually disciplining, or fussing. Remember, young children see everything as open territory to explore and do not distinguish between what is off limits.

For the safety of a child or another person, some things must, of course, be considered off limits. You will need to get a child's full attention and help him remember that certain things are not to be touched. If you keep the off-limits list as short as possible, your little ones are more likely to remember the restrictions.

Demand Good Manners

Insist on good manners. Good manners teach so many qualities inherent in the Christian worldview. For example:
- Respect for others.
- Concern for others.
- A kinder and gentler spirit.

Most of us balk inwardly at being ordered around. I believe we need to teach good manners as well as demonstrate them to our students. Verbalizations that get more mileage out of our students may include:

"You may clean up the centers now." (Instead of "Clean the centers now!")

"Please put the napkin and plate from your snack in the trash." (Instead of "Pick up your trash!")

I believe children should be trained, required, and reminded to use good manners, including using words such as "please," "thank you," and "excuse me."

Display Humor

Why is displaying humor an important principle of discipline? Because without humor, on many days, you could certainly lose your perspective entirely. Some days you simply have to step back, take a deep breath, and pray for the Lord to show you the humor in some situations. With little children, I sometimes say, "Did you eat wiggle worms for breakfast? I know you must have had silly cereal." With older students, I may say, "Is this my life or am I living in a sitcom, because I am more than ready for a commercial break from this!" Kids enjoy seeing adults find humor in situations, and it reminds us not to take certain situations or ourselves too seriously.

Dignify Each Child

God has made each child with a special personality, as well as individual strengths and weaknesses. Sometimes children may challenge or rattle us. So how do we dignify and encourage each student, even when we feel these emotions?

The answer here also lies in prayer. When we turn to the Lord to help us, it is amazing to see what He can, and will, do. So many times the Lord has given me grace and love for my students when I did not spontaneously feel gracious or loving. He has helped me find something to praise each child for on a daily basis.

Remember that children have feelings. They take orders and criticism from adults all day. If we had to absorb all of the verbal, emotional, and/or physical abuse that some children have to tolerate, we would be crushed. Make every effort not to crush their little spirits.

Preserve the dignity of each child, even in a situation where he disobeyed and must be disciplined. Choose your words carefully so that you enable children to maintain their dignity as you help them to develop Christlike character.

If we had to absorb all the verbal, emotional, and/or physical abuse that some of our students tolerate, we would be crushed.

Disciplining Each Personality

Now that we've gone over the various principles of discipline, let's take a look at how these principles apply specifically to your students. The more you understand about your students' temperaments and learning modalities, the more effective your discipline will be.

Choleric Curtis

This is the child from whom you can expect frequent disobedience. Sanguine Siena may be sassy, Melancholy Mei Li may be moody, but Curtis usually wants control at any cost. This temperament requires continual, strong discipline. Don't be discouraged if you lose some battles, but do work hard to win the war—which is to develop Christlike character.

Our own temperaments influence how we view the process of disciplining our students. A sanguine teacher may try to talk the choleric child out of his behavior or try to win him to her side with a pleasing personality. A melancholy teacher will try to control by attempting to teach in the perfect way. The choleric teacher will discipline the choleric child in full force, matching will for will. The best way to discipline the choleric child is to encourage him to take charge of his own behavior, and then help him channel all of his energy into becoming a strong, competent person. Let's look at a few behaviors you might witness in a choleric child as well as possible consequences for each behavior.

> **Your own temperament affects how you view the process of disciplining your students.**

Behavior:

Tries to control everyone and everything around him.

Consequence:

"You may be in charge of . . ." (Give specific tasks.)

You really can't tire these children out. In terms of ordering everyone else around, you may say, "I am the teacher. I make those decisions. But you may be in charge of helping me . . ."

Behavior:

Deliberate disobedience

Consequence:

He must be punished for this. Ask him, "What do you think would be an appropriate punishment? Obviously, if he chooses an inappropriate response, the decision comes back to you. Don't give away proper teacher control, but do delegate some to him when he shows he is ready.

Sanguine Siena

This is the child who is fun loving, talkative, and forgetful. Because of these tendencies, Siena will often get into trouble. She is not usually willfully disobedient—just forgetful. Children with this temperament need to suffer the pain of some logical consequences in order to learn a lesson.

Behavior:

Continual interruptions and constant chattering.

Consequence:

Start a checklist. Every time she interrupts or chatters, she receives a check. Each check results in five minutes of lost time doing a special activity.

Make sure that your consequences are tied to the behavior or it will not result in changed behavior. For example, many teachers simply move children to time out. While I think there is a time and place for time out, use it sparingly. For example, my son is a basketball coach at our school. He videotapes the games and studies them for hours as he writes up the drills for the next day. If he came to practice and said, "Hey, you all didn't play well, you must all go to time out for the entire practice." Would this change the behaviors? No! It is easy to see in this example why time outs don't always work, and yet it is what we as teachers often do. We need to use the consequences that are tied to the behavior to change the behavior.

Behavior:

Forgetting to turn in an assignment

Consequence:

She still has to do the assignment and turn it in but gets points taken off.

Behavior:

Saying things that are inappropriate and/or silly, just to get a response.

Consequence:

Have her state the information properly. Remember, practice drills are important for some children. They simply may not know the appropriate way to say something. Let's show them and have them practice it.

Behavior:

Monopolizing a class discussion.

Consequence:

Be put on "silence mode" for a certain amount of time.

You need to be sensitive to the fact that each temperament type will have tendencies toward certain behaviors; however, some of these behavior tendencies, if untamed, can haunt children for their entire lives. It is much better to tame them early than watch them produce a lifetime of painful consequences.

Also keep in mind that you respond to your students' personalities from the realm of your own temperament tendencies. You become a mirror through which a child sees himself. For example, a sanguine teacher may think his sanguine student is funny, cute, and adorable; therefore, the sanguine teacher may not want to discipline the child when she talks continually or does silly, yet disruptive, things. Thus, the result of this child receiving acceptance from the teacher can become a liability in terms of training that child into more mature behavior. If, on the other hand, you are a serious melancholy, this tendency of your sanguine student may drive you nuts, and you may be continually sending the child a nonverbal message that says, "You're not OK. Get serious about things."

In terms of discipline, Sanguine Siena needs fun! So discipline with humor and games. Yikes! I can almost hear some of you saying, "Did I read this wrong? Is Jody out of her mind? What do you mean, I should discipline with humor and games?" It's true! It really can be effective. For example, when you need the classroom cleaned up after a busy hands-on lesson, if you say: "Clean up this room now!" Sanguine Siena will not hear you, and then you'll have to deal with a potentially disobedient child. But if you say: "I wonder if we can get this all cleaned up by the time I count to 10," the results will differ dramatically. "I wonder" sounds like a game, and games must be fun! Therefore, sanguine children will respond more positively.

With young children it is easy to make just about everything into a game. (See *The Discipline Guide for Children's Ministry* by Jody Capehart & Gordon & Becki West.) With older students it is wiser to say "Let's get our room in order and if we can do so quickly, I have a special game for you." The game I have found that they enjoy the most is, "Wheel of Scripture."

"Wheel of Scripture" is an easy game to play with students in grades 3–6. It is an especially great game for grades 4–6 who have outgrown what they perceive as childish games. It is easy to play and to have everything you need at your disposal. Group your students, girls against boys. The boys will, of course, graciously let the girls go first. A girl spins, and if the spinner lands on a number, she guesses a letter. If the letter is part of the Bible passage that you have selected, you write the letter(s) in the appropriate spot on the game board. The girls team can either try and guess the passage or spin. If she lands on 0, or guesses a letter that isn't in the passage, or guesses the wrong passage, the boys get a turn. Continue back and forth until a team correctly guesses the passage.

If you want to get fancy, you can build a game board like the one on the Wheel of Fortune television program. You can build a stand with boards that have hooks to hang the letters. The spinner can be on a large stand so the student has to physically stand up to spin it.

Over the years, however, I have discovered ways to make this game budget friendly. Simply use a small spinner from a child's game. Take the largest sticky notes you can find and write the letters on them and attach them to your white board or a bulletin board. REMEMBER: the letters need to be on the inside of the paper, face down. OR you can simply put up blank papers and as students guess a letter, write it in with a large marker.

Students love this game, it teaches them and it is easy to use.

Phlegmatic Patrick

Phlegmatic children are very easygoing. Their need for discipline will usually show up as stubbornness or laziness. As a general rule, keep in mind that these children appear to be so easygoing that you often don't see many problems. However, some areas of frustration may include the following:

Behavior:

Passive-aggressive resistance to doing tasks: "Oh sure, I just forgot. I'll go do it now." (One hour later the task is still not done.)

Consequence:

If older, allow him to reap the natural consequences. If younger, enforce appropriate punishment when a task is not completed within a defined time. If the unattended task only affected him, he needs to go do it and reap the consequences of not doing something else he wants to do for that hour. If his neglect affects other students and this is becoming a habit, you may need to take away privileges. This is a time when the no pain, no gain rule applies.

Behavior:

Stubbornness as a quiet way of resisting authority.

Consequence:

Talk about it, helping the child to see it and to understand how it can be sin. Then define appropriate consequences if a child persists in this behavior.

When disciplining phlegmatic children, define the inappropriate behavior and put time parameters on tasks. Otherwise, their sweet, easygoing natures may lead them to let things slide, resulting in negative habits. Allowing phlegmatic children to reap the natural consequences of their behavior as they grow older becomes the most effective way to change those behaviors. Phlegmatics resent being pushed by anyone, especially cholerics.

Don't rescue them. Let them see the need to change their own behavior. Discipline is a discipling process. We want it to change behavior and not just be a quick fix. Since these children are sometimes

stubborn, they take their sweet time in cleaning up. A logical consequence would be to have them complete the task and miss the next
activity. For example, if you are cleaning up your centers to move on to
an art activity or story time, and the child does his passive aggressive
thing and doesn't clean up, calmly say, "When you are finished cleaning up, then you may join us." That puts the ball back into his court,
and he will learn that he must obey or he will miss something he likes.

Melancholy Mei Li

Mei Li is generally not a deliberately disobedient child, unless
perhaps she is part choleric. Discipline for the melancholy child
should deal more in the realm of moods or movements. By moods,
I am referring to the melancholy moods that can at times be overwhelming: "I can't go back to Sunday school because no one likes
me." Or "I can't learn long division, it's too hard."

For younger children you may get the melodrama of not wanting to be left by their parents. While a certain amount of fear and
anxiety may be natural, these children are experts in going over
the top. We need to reflect their feelings and assure them in a
calm voice, and then ignore them if they want to be a con-
tender for the Drama King or Queen. For example, I say,
"I can see that you are sad that Mommy and Daddy have
gone to church. They are right over there (point) and
they will be coming back to get you (point to the clock).
When the big hand gets to here and the little hand gets to
here, they will be back for you. Now I have something very
special to share with you. Will you be my Happy Helper? You
can show me by putting away the tears and putting on that
happy face."

Melancholies generally overstate things, usually in a
strongly negative tone. These children are overly sensitive and often very conscientious; therefore, when we
attempt to discipline them, they may become overwhelmed if we are not careful about our choice of words
and actions. Melancholies generally respond well to
quiet, relaxed words, which call attention to the
problem and suggest an appropriate solution.
Remember that melancholies sometimes
move to a different drummer, and this drummer is very slow. Part of this is caused by the
"melancholy freeze." This is what happens when the
perfectionist melancholy looks at the task needing to be accom-

plished, sees the ideal or perfect way to complete it, and begins to wonder how to attain that perfection. She begins to doubt herself and thus freezes and cannot function. You need to help her begin the task in order to get the inertia going and unlock the freeze. In other words, you must defrost her into action.

Here are some behaviors your melancholy child may manifest and what you can do about them:

Behavior:

"I'm not ready . . ." (takes forever to complete a task.)

Consequence:

Gently move in the perimeters: "In 10 minutes we will be finishing our papers."

Behavior:

Doesn't turn in a project because it is not good enough.

Consequence:

It's time for some cause and effect. "I think your project is wonderful. However, if you choose to not turn it in, here are the consequences . . ."

Discipline as Discipleship

Each of us is different, created uniquely for God's purpose. God has given you your students as a part of His purpose. He entrusts your students to you so that you may disciple them and help them to be the very best that they can be. Proper discipline is inherent in the discipleship process. It takes time, patience, prayer, and the Word. There are no pat answers. What works for one child may not work for another. That is why you must view discipline as a spiritual process, strive to be consistent with the Word, demonstrate the love of Christ, and be open to the guidance of the Holy Spirit.

Appropriate Classroom Discipline

Small Group Discussion

Answer the following questions to learn more about how you can formulate your own system of discipline based on the suggestions offered in this chapter.

1. Discuss the true meaning and purpose of discipline.

2. Divide into groups by the ages you teach and make a list of three issues that you deal with that require discipline procedures.
- First, role-play handling a student's discipline problem by reacting in the flesh and then by responding in the power of the Holy Spirit.
- Second, come up with an appropriate consequence for each behavior if the child continues in it.
- Make a chart. Remember the guidelines for appropriate consequences!

Inappropriate Behavior	Consequence
a.	
b.	
c.	

3. What are some ways you can redirect your students' energy in productive ways?

4. List three rules that you can use in your classroom:

-
-
-

5. Why are manners so important for the classroom?

6. How does the power of prayer affect how you view discipline?

7. Create a graphic organizer based on the sample shown on the next page. In the center of the graphic organizer place an issue that you deal with in your classroom that consistently takes up your time. Show how this can be most effectively dealt with for each of the different learners. In other words, to what methods does each learner best respond in terms of discipline?

Small Group Discussion (Continued)

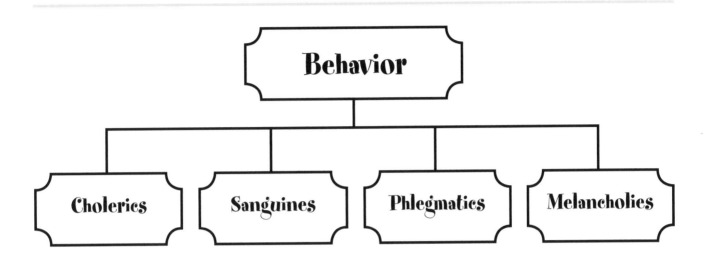

8. Create a picture in your mind of your discipline system. Ask yourself the following questions:

Is it clear?

Is it consistent?

Is it Christlike?

9. What are age-appropriate means of obtaining quiet in the classroom through:

Non-verbal cues

Songs

Games

10. Why is the relationship between the teacher and the student so important? What are other ways that you can build positive relationships with your students?

11. Make a sound meter for your classroom. Try it for a month and review its effectivess.

Disciplining Each Personality

Fill in the spaces below. Then review which forms of discipline work best for each personality.

Choleric Curtis: This temperament requires _____ , strong discipline.

- Don't be discouraged if you lose some battles, but do work hard to win the war to develop Christlike character.
- The best way to discipline this child is to encourage him to take charge of his own behavior without giving away teacher control.
- If he tries to control his surroundings, give him specific tasks to be in charge of.
- If he responds in deliberate disobedience he must be disciplined.

Sanguine Siena: Children with this temperament need to suffer the pain of some logical _____ to learn a lesson.

- This child is not usually willfully disobedient, just forgetful.
- She needs fun so discipline with humor and with games.
- If she continually interrupts start a checklist of her behavior to keep her on track.
- If she starts to say inappropriate things to get a response, ask her to state the information properly—practice drills are important for sanguine children.

Phlegmatic Patrick: Children with this temperament will show a need for discipline in the form of _____ or laziness.

- For phlegmatic children, define the inappropriate behavior and put time parameters on tasks.
- Allowing him to reap the natural consequences of his behavior is the most effective way to change the behavior.
- If he responds to you with passive-aggressive resistance, allow him to reap the consequences when the task is not done.
- If he responds with stubbornness, talk to him and help him to see his resisting authority as disobedience and sin.

Melancholy Mei Li: Children with this temperament need discipline in the realm of _____ or movements.

- For these children it is important to reflect their feelings back to them.
- Because Melancholy Mei Li is very sensitive and conscientious, attempts to discipline her may overwhelm her if the words and actions are not chose carefully—use quiet, relaxed words that call attention to the problem and suggest an appropriate solution.
- If she gives in to the "melancholy freeze" and takes forever to complete a task, gently move in the parameters and let her know how much time she has left.
- If she cannot complete projects due to "paralysis of analysis" (she thinks her work is not good enough), encourage her that she has made a great effort, give her the option of not turning it in, and inform her of the consequences if she chooses not to complete the work.

Discipline Reminders

Keep the following points in mind when deciding on your system of discipline:

- Depend on the Holy Spirit and prayer.
- Define and discuss your basic system with your students.
- Make sure that the consequences are tied in with the behavior, or it will not result in changed behavior.
- Be careful not to discipline according to your own personality type, but discipline according to the personalities of your students.
- Be willing to try new systems of discipline in your classroom.

Remember that the ultimate goal of discipline is discipleship!

Chapter 10

Cherishing and Challenging Children Through Christlike Communication

A Teacher with HEART is a caring communicator who creates a learning climate that is conducive to helping children grow in character, content, and conduct.

Scripture: "But the fruit of the Spirit is love, joy, peace, patience, kindness, goodness, faithfulness, gentleness and self-control. Against such things there is no law" (Galatians 5:22, 23).

Teaching Objective: To use communication to build bridges to Christ and not to create roadblocks.

> "You" messages create roadblocks . . .
> "I" messages build bridges.

Verbal Communication

Children are very sensitive; they feel what we are thinking about them. Sometimes it may be we who are having a hard day, but children may feel they have caused it. We must talk with them and carefully articulate what is happening and how we truly feel.

You may be asking, "But what if I really am upset with a child? Will my words hurt his self-esteem?" It is best to communicate authentically. But our words can hurt, so we must select them with care. When we begin to discuss a sensitive issue by saying, "You" the other person is immediately on the defensive. But when we claim responsibility for how we feel, using "I" messages, then the other person can listen in greater comfort. For example, we could say, "You never listen to me . . ." But we should say, "I feel hurt when I tell you to do something and you ignore me," or "I feel frustrated when I have to stop and tell you to be quiet so that I can teach you." "I" messages build bridges for understanding whereas "you" messages become roadblocks to communication. To avoid these roadblocks, focus on developing good communication with children by practicing bridge-building techniques.

Communication roadblocks include:

- Moralizing: "You shouldn't . . ." or "If you were a good Christian, you wouldn't . . . "
- Analyzing: "You always say that when you don't want to do something."
- Judging: "What a dumb thing to say."
- Labeling: "You're acting like you have a learning problem."
- Threatening: "If you don't . . . I will . . . "
- Advising: "You should have done it the way I told you."
- Sarcasm: "So you think you're pretty smart."

Bridge-building communication techniques include:

- Focusing on the action the child performed not the character of the child: "You did a great job on this project."
- Focusing on the child's attitude, not always the end result of his behavior: "I can see you tried hard, and I am really proud of you for trying so hard."
- Assuming the best in your students: "I can see you started to clean up your clutter. Let's see, which gets put away next."

Communication is the invisible glue that can mend relationships or sticky them up.

An Environment for Communication

Before we look at the actual words we use with children, let's examine the environment that we have provided. Is the emotional climate of the classroom conducive to caring communication? As I mentioned earlier, the unspoken communication of feelings can set the tone for the room. If the words we use don't match the feel of the room, children will become very confused. Therefore, the first step is to clear the air of any emotional baggage. In other words, let there be authenticity between what you feel and what you say.

The second step is to set aside time for practicing good communication with your students. I feel very strongly about this and elaborate on it in Chapter 8. Children learn to be good communicators by participating in good communication processes, which include opportunities to talk and listen.

Some children chatter nonstop, and it can become easy to tune them out. However, when they're older we want to know what they are thinking, and they cease to talk. The way to help prevent this withdrawal is to form positive patterns of communication in children's lives.

Model Caring Communication

One of the best ways to teach children to become caring communicators is to model such behavior ourselves. Let's examine some of the guidelines for caring communication by addressing the following questions:

- Am I being a channel of God's love?

    I challenge you to turn on a taperecorder and record a typical conversation between you and your students on one of those challenging days. Later, take a box of tissues and sit down to listen. Listen first for the tone, and then the climate. Then make two lists and pick out key words you communicated that were hurtful and those that were caring.

    In stressful situations it is so easy to revert back to old expressions that we heard when we were children. Often we have no conscious awareness that we use them. We have to do some careful cleaning out of our communication before we can be a channel of God's love.

    What else must we do to be a channel of God's love? How can we converse in ways that best communicate love? First, we must go to the dictionary of God's love, His Word. We find much there that will help us. Take a moment to look

Let there be authenticity between what you feel and what you say.

up the following verses in your Bible and make some notes about what each verse has to say about ways of speaking.

| Proverbs 10:31, 32 | Proverbs 15:1 |
| Proverbs 18:7 | Ephesians 4:29 |

We must pray to be a channel of Christ's love. As we pray for a heart and a mouthpiece overflowing with His love, He begins to fill us with His Spirit. That is one of the greatest joys of being a Christian. There is hope! The old can fall away and the new can be built. "Therefore, if anyone is in Christ, he is a new creation; the old has gone, the new has come!" (2 Corinthians 5:17).

- Am I living as a Spirit-controlled Christian?

The Holy Spirit not only fills us with His words, but he also begins to put a check on our impulses. Instead of being a motor-mouth who has to go back and apologize, we can be Spirit-controlled. There is joy in being around a Spirit-controlled Christian. You feel it. You sense it. You desire it.

Being Spirit-controlled means that we can make a conscious decision to act instead of always reacting. Instead of bouncing back like a hastily tossed rubber ball, we can begin to control our responses. For example, when I am feeling impulsive and am apt to get myself in trouble, I try to do nothing—which is very hard for me. I force myself to stop, look, and listen. Meanwhile, inside I'm fervently praying, "Holy Spirit, help! Take over! Quick!" I muzzle-mouth (Psalm 39:1) myself until I feel His indwelling presence working through me. God is ever faithful. He has promised the gift of His Holy Spirit. He is your forever friend. He wants to help you. Call on Him! "But the Counselor, the Holy Spirit, whom the Father will send in my name, will teach you all things and will remind you of everything I have said to you" (John 14:26).

- Are my words characteristic of Jesus?

Over the years I have often asked myself, "How would Jesus handle this? What would Jesus say?" I always invite Him to be the unseen guest at parent conferences, staff meetings, and chapel. His very presence changes the climate of any room. We certainly would not act or talk ugly with Him there. This verbalization works well with children also. You can put a chair in the classroom with a sign on it that says, JESUS. Remind the children that Jesus is always with us even if we can't see Him.

Pray for a heart and mouthpiece overflowing with His love.

- Are my words considerate of my students' feelings?

  When a child has the wrong answer don't simply say, "No, that's not right. Who has the right answer?" Instead say, "Thank you for answering the question, who has another thought?" If we put children down when they answer incorrectly they will quit trying or revert to using silliness to cover up their embarrassment. Other statements that would also work include, "I think you had the right answer; you just forgot. It happens to me as well." Or "You are on the right track, let's see what ideas other people have as well."

- Do my words convey how much I cherish my children and my coworkers?

  Use statements such as the following to convey a cherishing attitude toward your students: "I love coming to teach you. You are such a kind class and you bless me so much." "You have such wonderful parents and I am enjoying getting to know them." "God gave us a very special and beautiful gift when he gave you to us." "You bless our class so much with your sense of humor." " I love to hear you play the piano."

- Do my words contribute to calm or chaos in my classroom?

  When we speak softly and gently it helps our children to speak that way too. When I speak calmly and quietly to my students during hurried times, it helps them remain calm and focused. If I say, "Hurry! Hurry!" and I am agitated, I am just adding to the chaos. Proverbs 15:1 reminds us, "A gentle answer turns away wrath, but a harsh word stirs up anger."

- Am I composed?

  Once again we need the Holy Spirit to help us by growing in us the spiritual fruit of "love, joy, peace, patience, kindness, goodness, faithfulness, gentleness and self-control" (Galatians 5:22, 23). When we confess a bad attitude and pray for His help, grace abounds. We find strength and peace to handle daily trials and frustrations.

- Am I cheerful?

  Practice using a cheerful voice with your students and see what happens. We can change a whole situation around for the better simply by changing our tone of voice and the words we use to express ourselves. A statement like, "I feel overwhelmed when there are lots of things out of place" will get me much further with the students than demanding, "Why can't you ever put things away?"

- Do I show concern for each student and staff member? Is it reflected in my tone of voice as well as in my words?

     For example:

     "I know it's hard to memorize all this, but if we keep trying, we will feel so good." "I bet it was hard to be in school when your new baby brother cried all night." Or "I know you get a headache on days you have a substitute teacher. Let's talk about it."

     We must try hard not to add the 25 cent lecture: "If you worked harder, you would have done better on this project." Or "This is the 19th paper you've lost this year. Why can't you . . .?" Try compassion. It builds positive communication.

- Do I compliment the children's efforts a well as achievements?

     It's their character that's most important. Some children are gifted achievers, but if we continually praise their achievements, their character development may lag. When we praise children for godly character or for trying to be Christlike, we build in them strength of character.

     Be cautious about such statements as, "You're such a good boy," or "You're always sweet." A child starts thinking, "If she knew the truth about me, she wouldn't say that." Anxiety sets in. Praise the deed, the effort, or the character displayed.

     For example:

     "I liked the way you shared your colored pencils with the new student" (deed).

     "I know you worked hard on cleaning your center"(effort).

     "I am proud of you for telling the truth even though you knew it might get you into trouble" (character).

- Are my words constructive?

     Some people love to criticize and control and thus can rationalize all their criticism as being constructive. But in reality, criticism can hurt deeply and children often receive a great deal of it. The tenacity of a 2-year-old is often diminished by the onslaught of well meaning criticism from adults.

     For example:

     "Now say it better, Johnny. Slow down. Come on Johnny . . . " Instead say, "Thank you Johnny for answering the question." Ignore any mispronunciations or stuttering. Praise the effort.

- Am I specific in what I seek to communicate to my students?

     The best advice is this: never assume. In a school were I served as principal, the classrooms were built around a court-yard. During cold weather we sometimes allowed the kinder-

Praising children for Christlike behavior builds strength of character.

garten children to go through one of the high school rooms as a warmer way to go to the rest rooms on the other side of the building instead of through the courtyard. One particular day I had to inform the kindergarten children that they could not use that access route. I went over the reason and procedure very carefully and closed with "Now children, remember: when you need to go to the rest room, you must go outside around the courtyard."

Later I was in my office which overlooks the courtyard, and to my dismay, saw a child squatting in the courtyard while his line partner tried to guard his dignity. I hurried out to find out why this child was using our beautiful courtyard as his personal rest room. He must have noted the look on my face because as I approached he said, "But Mrs. Capehart you said if we needed to use the rest room to go outside around the courtyard!" I had to smile. So much for clear and concise communication. I brought him inside, apologized for not being more specific, and we all survived the experience. I was once again reminded of how very important clear communication is!

Another favorite story of mine is the one about a 4-year-old sanguine child who never listened in chapel but always talked about his adventures at Grandma's, the zoo, the park, etc. He had an uncanny ability to sidetrack any chapel lesson. Therefore, I often chose not to call on him during critical times in chapel such as during the gospel presentation. I knew he would take us on a quick detour to Grandma's or a favorite TV show.

During one chapel message I taught the children John 14:2: In my Father's house are many rooms . . . I am going there to prepare a place for you." I was just preparing to give the gospel message when his hand shot up. I groaned inwardly, trying to ignore his hyperventilating and hand waving. Finally, I took a deep breath and called on him.

He said, in his 4-year-old voice, "Mrs. Capehart, Jesus can fix anything right?" I was in shock. He was reasonably close to the right topic.

Another deep breath, "Yes dear. Why do you ask?"

"Well, the Bible says Jesus said, 'I go to *repair* a place for you." Once again, I learned the importance of clarity in communication.

Creative Storytelling

Becoming a Storyteller

Our children are bombarded today with visual images and not always with the ones we want them to see. At the rare times when I go to a movie, I often cringe over the previews. Even if a movie has a good rating (and even that is relative today), the previews are often total scum. Even if a parent screens the television programs, the commercials are contrary to our Christian message. Unfortunately, these visual images stay with children. It seems that the world of visual imagery is something the media has discovered how to use quite well and the church can't afford to leave this resource untapped.

Teachers used to use storytelling as the way to pass on stories of faith. Children had to listen to get it. But now there is much that is communicated visually, and those images are imprinted in the minds of our children. Visual images, good or bad, have staying power. We see children with learning issues in auditory processing, and I believe that many of these deficits are culturally induced.

Children today do not have the language skills that are needed to succeed in school. Brain research and brain scans show us what is happening in the area of language development in the brain. When children have not received sufficient adult interaction in verbal areas, including one-on-one communication, there are areas of the brain that do not develop properly. We are raising our children on sound bites, "McThoughts" if you will, instead of rich, intelligent adult conversation and interaction.

The art of storytelling needs to be a part of every classroom taught by a teacher with HEART. Creative storytelling can build positive visual images that will reinforce biblical truths while helping children develop language skills and the art of listening. Here are my top 10 ways to make the most of communication through storytelling:

1. Pray about what you are communicating so that the message you want to come through will be there.
2. Know your story so that you are relaxed telling it.
3. Use great voice inflection. With young children you can be exaggerated. They love it! At first older children will think you are weird, but with humor you can say, "I knew you would think I sound weird. Would you like to try doing the voices?" Sometimes they will say yes. At other times they will say, "No, you can do it." But if you acknowledge it ahead of time, they are OK with exaggerated voice inflection. Remember, being "cool" is everything to older children. The truth is they love storytelling, but be prepared for them to act like they don't.
4. Believe in the credibility of the story yourself.

5. Help your students visualize the setting. You may even have them close their eyes. Other children may like to draw as you tell the story. Let them choose how they get into it.

6. Describe the characters in depth so they feel as if they know the person. Sometimes I dress up as the main character or put on different hats to represent each character.

7. Ask questions along the way to see if they are truly with you. Don't drill them, but do involve them.

For example:

"How do you think he feels right now?"

"Have you ever felt that way?"

"What do you think will happen next?"

   If it is a longer story that will take several days (school setting) or weeks (church setting), always end with a cliffhanger. Child Evangelism Fellowship has great missionary stories that set this up for you in an excellent way. (See the bibliography at the end of this book for the best way to contact your local CEF.)

8. Help the students to think concepts through to develop critical thinking skills.

9. Focus on involving the different learning styles by how you tell the story:

   "Visualize a beautiful waterfall."

   "Can you hear the water? What does it sound like? Can you smell it?"

   "Can you imagine standing in it? How would it feel?"

"Would you feel afraid? Would you be excited?"

10. Divide the class into groups, and allow them to develop a conclusion to the story or even to develop their own stories to share with the other groups.

Here are some examples of how to use storytelling both in church and in the Christian classroom.

The following example shows how storytelling can be an effective tool in communicating the gospel to children. Say: "Today we are going to read a Scripture story from Luke 8:22-25. This is a story about Jesus with the disciples in a boat when a storm comes up unexpectedly. Let's take our chairs and make them into a pretend boat. Let's make-believe that we are the disciples in the boat with Jesus. We are very calm and peaceful. The boat is rocking gently, in fact so gently that we are slowly falling asleep. (Make your voice slow, soft, and soothing.) Suddenly the wind starts to blow. It wakes you up! You are so surprised that a storm is here because it

---

Questions, Questions, and More Questions

Rather than ask review questions that simply restate the obvious, ask questions that challenge your students to look for ways to relate the story to their lives. Jesus asked thought-provoking questions that helped listeners discover the point of the story for themselves.

Excerpt from *Sharable Parables* by Steven James. Standard Publishing, 2005.

was so calm when you drifted off to sleep. Can you hear it? Can you feel it? We are starting to tip back and forth in the boat. Let's make our bodies tip back and forth in the boat. The disciples cried out "Master, Master, we are going to drown!" (v. 24). Can you hear them crying out to Jesus? Why? What were they feeling? What do you feel like doing when you are afraid? Jesus stood up and told the wind to be still and it was. Isn't that amazing? Even the wind obeys Jesus. Can you think of a time when things were very loud and scary but you knew that Jesus was with you? How did you feel? Encourage discussion and relate it to the personal life experiences of the children.

In a school setting a story may not always have a biblical or moral tone. For example, before I teach long division, I tell the students this story to capture their attention, as well as to teach a consistent mathematical principle of long division:

"Let me tell you a story. On a particular planet there live Martians, and Martians love green apples. Now the monarch of this planet believes in quiet, order, and peace—just as we do in our classroom. So he dictated the following decree: 'Whatever one Martian gets, they all get.'

"So here are four Martians. (I put out four green skittles to represent the four Martians.) Here are eight green apples. (I use eight beads. You can draw this on the white board with a green marker also.) Let's give one green apple to each Martian. (Some children may know the answer, of course, but still proceed.) Here's one for this Martian, one for this Martian . . ." (Proceed in sequence.)

"Finally, how many did each Martian get? Yes! Here is an important rule in division, the answer is always what the one Martian got." (Yes, this is simple stuff, but if you proceed up to three digits in the division, the answer is still what the one received.)

Storytelling is an effective technique for teaching all kinds of concepts, and children of all ages love stories. As Christians, I believe we need to follow the biblical mandates as stated in Deuteronomy 6:6-9 to make use of every opportunity as a teaching tool to share the Word of God with our students. Let us communicate the commandments of God as we teach our students to see them, talk about them, touch them, and put them into practice.

Growing faith in our students is the goal of our teaching. We aim to pass our faith from our generation to the next. Let us be diligent in how we share our faith with this generation so that they will, in turn, continue in passing on their faith to others.

Four Keys to Opening Yourself Up to Storytelling

Key One: Open Your Heart

Jesus said, "For out of the overflow of the heart the mouth speaks" (Matthew 12:34).

As we prepare to share stories with the children we teach, we need to remember that the first step is to open up our hearts to God. We have His promise that His Word will not return to Him without being effective (Isaiah 55:10, 11). When you prayerfully prepare your lessons, you're not alone! You can rely on the person and power of the Holy Spirit to impact the lives of your listeners when you're faithful in telling the stories of God.

Care about the story you're learning. Find a personal connection to it. If you're not passionate about learning and telling the story, your lack of zeal will show through to the audience.

Key Two: Open Your Mind

"After three days they found him in the temple courts, sitting among the teachers, listening to them and asking them questions" (Luke 2:46).

"Then he opened their minds so they could understand the Scriptures (Luke 24:45).

Even as a boy, Jesus was serious about learning God's Word. He opened His mind to God. Later, when He became a teacher, He still used stories and questions to inspire reflection in His followers.

Opening your mind to God means being a serious student of His Word. It also means embracing and fostering imagination and taking your job of learning stories seriously. God wants to be the one fueling our passions and igniting our dreams. He wants us to let go of our safeguards, trust wholly in His promises, and open our minds to the truth of His Word!

Key Three: Open Your Eyes

Solomon noticed things. He was an astute observer of life. His dad (King David) was one of the nation's foremost poets and musicians and, like his dad, Solomon was always on the lookout for truth and for parallels between everyday situations and spiritual lessons. He knew that spiritual truth may be found everywhere, if only we have the eyes to see it.

One day, as Solomon was looking out the window, he saw a married woman flirting with a man other than her husband. He used this illustration from everyday life to teach the importance of fidelity and purity (Proverbs 7:6-27). Throughout Ecclesiastes, he lists other observations and the lessons he learned from them.

Like Solomon, an effective Christian storyteller is always on the lookout for stories that reflect truth. Notice the pattern Solomon followed: First, he would carefully observe a situation. Then he would reflect on it and consider parallels to scriptural truth. Finally, he would apply the story or situation to life. Open your eyes to the stories around you.

Key Four: Open Your Ears

Jesus said, "He who has ears, let him hear" (Matthew 13:9). An effective storyteller is observant, both toward the story he is telling, and toward his listeners. Even though it might sound strange, a storyteller listens to himself, his story, and his audience during the storytelling event. How does a storyteller listen to the audience? By observing the body language of the listeners, and then responding to how they respond to the story! So open your ears, listen, and respond.

Excerpt from *The Creative Storytelling Guide* by Steven James. Standard Publishing, 2002.

Communicate with Silence

The Value of Silence

Silence is a lost art in our culture. I have been saddened to see that the trends in church education have often followed too closely the trends in culture. Children need a balance between exciting, active learning experiences and silence, in which they can learn to listen for the still, small voice of God (1 Kings 19:11-13).

There is definite value of making learning fun for children. If you have heard me speak or have read my other books you know that I believe in fun, creative, active learning. But I also believe in the profound value of silence.

Let me illustrate this point. Before I begin teaching a class or leading children in worship, I provide time for quiet and silence. With young children (up to 3rd grade), I may say, "Let's play the silence game. Let us listen to the silence. What do you hear?" They may hear the air conditioning unit. Probably, they will hear nothing.

For worship time in church and for chapel in school, I have the lights turned down low. The children enter the room quietly. I sometimes have soft music playing. I wait until it is completely quiet, and then open in prayer. This sets a climate conducive to worship. I always begin and end in silence. In between you can provide a rich array of activities through music, games, storytelling, active learning, puppets, and drama. But may I please encourage you to train children in the art of silence. I have never found a group of children who do not respond positively to this.

Beloved teachers, do not give up heart. Continue to teach and communicate Christ with all your heart. You are called by divine appointment to teach. Teach with all your HEART so that you can pass along your faith to the next generation. You are called for such a time as this. Communicate Christ with your words, actions, prayers, body language, attitude, and in your silence.

How Do You Communicate?

Take time to reflect on all the aspects that make up good communication with children. Answer the following questions as you reflect on your own personal communication skills.

1. What are your real attitudes as you communicate? What are your real motives? Do you have hidden agendas?

2. Do you express how you really feel? What do your students feel from you?

3. Think about your actions. What do you actually do about what you say? Be sure that you actions are consistent with your words.

4. Write down some actual words that express the attitude of your heart and how you would like to communicate with children.

5. Memorize a few Bible verses that express the spirit of what you want your communication with children to be. Don't forget to pray about modeling good communication with children.

Christlike Communication

Tips for Christlike Communication

Fill in the spaces below. Then review these tips to learn how to become more Christlike in how you communicate with children.

I. _____ Communication
  a. Children feel what you are thinking. Talk with them carefully and clearly articulate your feelings.
  b. "I" messages build bridges whereas "you" messages become roadblocks to communication.
  c. Avoid communication roadblocks and focus on building bridges with your words.

II. An _____ for Communication
  a. Examine your environment. Is the emotional climate of the classroom conducive to caring communication?
  b. Let there be authenticity between what you feel and what you say.
  c. Set aside time for practicing good communication with your students. Children learn to be good communicators through opportunities to practice appropriate forms of talking and listening.

III. Model _____ Communication
  a. Your heart: Pray to be a channel of God's love, to live as a Spirit-controlled Christian, and to speak in a way that reflects the attitude of Christ.
  b. Your words: Use words that are considerate of your student's feelings, convey a cherishing attitude, and contribute to a calm classroom environment.
  c. Your attitude: Display a demeanor that is composed, cheerful, and shows concern for the children and adults you work with.
  d. Your actions: Compliment the efforts of your students, offer suggestions constructively, and be specific in what you aim to communicate to the children you teach.

IV. Creative _____
  a. Use visual images to reinforce biblical truths.
  b. Ask questions that will challenge your students and involve them in the story—teach as Jesus taught!
  c. Focus on making an effort to involve each learning style in your storytelling technique.

V. Communicate with _____
  a. Children need a balance between exciting, active learning experiences and silence, in which they can learn to listen for the still, small voice of God.
  b. Provide opportunities for children to practice silence.
  c. Communicate Christ with your words, actions, prayers, body language, attitude, and in your silence.

Chapter 11

Cherishing and Challenging Children to Build Healthy Self-Esteem

A Teacher with HEART finds ways to encourage, energize, and empower each child to be all he can be for Jesus Christ.

Scripture: "Do not let any unwholesome talk come out of your mouths, but only what is helpful for building others up according to their needs, that it may benefit those who listen" (Ephesians 4:29).

Teaching Objective: To find practical ways to create a classroom environment where students feel encouraged to be the best they can be, energized, and empowered with skills that utilize their strengths. To demonstrate for students the unconditional love of "Jesus Christ [who] is the same yesterday and today and forever" (Hebrews 13:8).

Building Healthy Self-Esteem

> Positive self-esteem is feeling confident that you can handle anything that comes your way.

Positive Self-Esteem

What is positive self-esteem? Positive self-esteem is feeling good about yourself. It is feeling important to someone who is important to you. It is feeling productive and confident that you can handle anything that comes your way. It is feeling purposeful and secure about reaching your goals. Self-esteem always expresses itself in the way you act, what you do, and how you behave.

So what are characteristics of positive self-esteem in children? What is this gift we hope to pass on to our students?

Children with positive self-esteem will be proud of their accomplishments. A young child may appear to be bragging on his accomplishments when, in reality, he is just being purely honest about how he feels: "Teacher, look at this neat picture that I painted."

They will handle their frustrations well. Children with a positive self-image will acknowledge that some things in life are truly tough, but they will keep trying. Perseverance is necessary for achieving success with small tasks as well as large tasks: "It's really hard to tie shoes, but I can do it."

They will assume responsibility. A child with high self-esteem will want to assume some responsibility:

"I'll help you."

"I did this project all by myself!"

"I got my church offering from my bank all by myself."

They will act independently and appropriately. A little child often says, "I do it myself." Children go through a stage of wanting to do things by themselves; however, they do not have the skills to do the things that they want to do. Then, about the time they acquire the skills, they lose the desire. That is precisely why I encourage teachers to train children in skills while the desire is strong. This will do wonderful things for self-esteem!

They will approach new challenges with enthusiasm: "Guess what? Tomorrow we are going to learn cursive. I can't wait!"

They will exhibit a broad range of emotions and feelings that are age appropriate. The key here lies in the word *appropriate*. For example, 4-year-olds are emotionally extreme. They laugh too hard, play too hard, and cry too hard. They love bathroom words. This is appropriate for this age. You still need to train them into appropriate behavior for maturity, but you must remember that they are manifesting appropriate behavior for their age and are not necessarily headed for juvenile hall (even though some days you do wonder). Now, if a 7-year-old child acted this way, such inappropriate behavior would need special attention.

They will feel that they have a degree of influence over their environment. Children with positive self-esteem can go into a situation where they know no one and yet feel confident they will make friends. Once again, temperament does play a part. A sanguine child will try to gain approval through a winning personality. A choleric child will use force to take control of the situation. A melancholy child will be overwhelmed and think that no one likes her and that she has no control over the situation. A phlegmatic child will observe quietly and peacefully from the sidelines and not get too uptight one way or the other.

I believe that each teacher brings to the classroom his own temperaments, gifts, learning style, and personality. As teachers, we need to be wise in training up our students. But we will make mistakes; therefore, the most important legacy we can give our students is to lead them to Jesus Christ, because it is through His sanctifying grace and forgiveness that children can grow beyond many of the mistakes with which we leave them.

Mirrors and Self-Esteem

Dorothy Briggs, in her excellent book, *Your Child's Self-Esteem* (1970) talks about the phenomena of the mirrors. She explains that children see themselves through a psychological mirror. They perceive who they are by the way the people around them respond to them. Children also see themselves through an insidious emotional mirror in which instated body language messages may be more powerful than overtly stated messages. For example, the patience or impatience we silently verbalize to our classroom speaks volumes to our students.

These mirrors become powerful mechanisms that help produce self-esteem. As babies and young children, we are powerless over them, yet all the while they are making us into who we will be.

Teachers often become the mirrors through which students see themselves. Our verbal and nonverbal expectations become the grid through which children filter their understanding of themselves. As Dorothy Briggs challenges in her book, we must find out where these expectations came from and whether or not they are valid. Are they borrowed? ("A quiet child is a good child.") Are they hangover wishes from our own childhood? Do we become determined that the children we encounter will receive what we longed for but did not experience as children?

Children look up to adults, and whatever we think is important, they will think is important. As Dorothy Briggs states, "Children

> **Instated body language messages may be more powerful than overtly stated messages.**

rarely question our expectations, instead, they question their personal adequacy" (Briggs 1975).

Viewing Children As Priceless, Not Worthless

In Dr. Dobson's excellent book on self-esteem, Hide or Seek (1974), he says that our society has two criteria for measuring self-worth: beauty and intelligence. He documents these two criteria so well that it is frightening to think of bringing a child into the world who does not possess these qualities.

I know that what he writes is true. As an educator I was determined to counteract this and to help each child see how very special he or she is. It thrilled me when I saw children whose self-image had been battered become healed and whole in our school.

It happened because we worked hard as a staff to do the following:

- Pray for and with each child.
- See each child as the individual God created him to be and teach him in that way.
- Love, touch, and affirm each child each day.

We need to pray that God will open our spiritual eyes to see our students as God created them to be and that He will enable us to embrace our students' unique qualities rather than force them into our mold. We also need to love, touch, and affirm each child in every encounter. It's easy to get in a hurry and just get through the day. But we need to make a conscious effort to look into our students' eyes and truly make contact. The world can be cruel to children, especially if they are a little different. In order to find a harbor in the storm of life, our children need the anchor of parents and teachers who love them unconditionally.

Children want to please their parents and teachers more than anything else in the world. And when they do something that yields approval, their self-esteem is naturally reinforced. If a child finds approval spontaneously and easily because he is exactly what his parents and teachers want him to be, a positive self-image is born. But pity the child who has jumped through every hoop, figuratively

> **Parents and teachers who love unconditionally offer a harbor for children in the storms of life.**

> **Positive experiences build positive behaviors. Negative experiences build defenses.**

speaking, and Mom, Dad, and teacher are still not happy. How his soul grieves. Instead of feeling priceless, he feels worthless. It hurts. And he begins the process of building defenses to ease the pain.

The child who receives approval for what he does, builds upon those experiences. Positive experiences build positive behaviors. Negative experiences build defenses.

This may seem strong, but in reality, these things do happen. When parents and teachers do not take time to look at their children as God created them, disaster can result.

ABC's of Self-Esteem

A Self-Esteem Improvement Plan

Now that we've examined what self-esteem is and how we affect our students' view of themselves, let's look at specific ways to help build the self-esteem of the children in your class.

A   Affirm your students.
Appreciate them as they are.

B   Believe in your students and communicate this to them.

C   Cherish and challenge your students.

D   Discipline them with loving fairness and consistency.

E   Encourage, energize, empower, and equip your students.

F   Follow through on what you say.

G   Godliness modeled is godliness gained—keep in mind that you are being watched!

H   Helping hands: God gave us hands to help one another.

I   Impart to your students how very important they are.

J   Joke with them; have fun!

K   Kindness is key! Treat them with kindness.

L   Listen, listen, listen to them!
Love, love, love them!

M   Mean what you say, and say what you mean.

N   Nurture your students.

O   Open your mind and attitude to the fact that God made your students differently from you and from each other.

P Praise your students sincerely.
Pray daily for your students and your relationship with them.

Q Quiet time is essential. Spend quiet time with your students.

R Reinforce their best attempts.

S Salvation—make it a matter of prayer for each of your students. Success builds success. Help students identify and build on their accomplishments.

T Teach them the Word of God and remain true to the Bible in all things.

U Uniqueness is a gift from God—cherish their differences.

V Victories come in small stages. Help your students find contentment with their level of progress.

W Welcome them into your class and into your life. Communicate to them that they have a special place in your heart.

X eXclude negative influences that will affect their character.

Y You. Give them the gift of your time and attention.

Z Zealously guard your tongue. Harsh words can crush a child's self-esteem.

Temperament and Self-esteem

All children need to have five basic needs met in order to feel good about themselves. (Actually, adults have the same needs.)

Part of: We all want to be part of something greater than ourselves. Pray for each child's salvation so that his need for connectedness will be met in Christ. He will feel a part in God's kingdom.

Position: Each child needs to feel unique and that he is No. 1 in being the best he can be. This comes from feeling appreciated and affirmed for his uniqueness. Cherish each child's differences as gifts from God.

Power: Each child needs to feel that he has the innate power to make a difference in the world. This feeling of power motivates him to try. A feeling of powerlessness results in apathy. Look at his God-given strengths and show him how to use his gifts for God. Say, "God has given you such a kind heart. When you show kindness to others, you are sharing God with them."

Peers and People: Who are the friends that surround each child? Who are the people she looks up to? We are all influenced, positively and negatively, by the people around us. Select children that would have a positive influence on a particular student and give him two choices of children to work with. For example: "You may work with Sarah or Samuel. Who do you choose?" (Sometimes if we force a single choice on a child, that child may reject the choice for that reason alone. But if we give the child a choice, he feels that he has more control.)

Positive Experiences: We all gravitate to where we feel good. If we don't feel good when we are with people or when we are part of something greater than us, then we may seek other influences such as drugs, food, or other pleasures of the world. Before the children are dismissed, a teacher can review the Sunday or school day by saying, "What are some positive things that happened today? Let's see if we can name three." You may think it is stating the obvious, but you may be surprised to find out what children view as the blessings of the day. Also it leaves them with a fresh memory of the positives to have as an answer when a parent asks, "What did you learn today?" And it will help prevent children from giving their typical answer: "Nothing."

Personality Preferences and Self-Esteem

An understanding of each child's temperament will greatly enhance your ability to meet the self-esteem needs of each child. The following chart is a tool to help you see the differences in your students in order to better understand, love, cherish, and challenge them.

	Choleric	Sanguine	Phlegmatic	Melancholy
Part of	Wants to be in charge of any group	Wants to be part of a group that approves of her and finds her adorable	Feels content with whatever life offers	Wants to be a part of something meaningful that is worth sacrificing for
Position	Can see whole picture and plug everyone into the parts	Is fun loving, enjoys being on stage performing	Feels OK about self, doesn't need to prove himself	Is perfectionistic, genius prone, musical, artistic
Power	Likes to run things, take charge, delegate	Performs for others' approval	May gain power by being stubborn	Insists on doing it right, doing it perfectly
Peers and People	Looks up to those in power greater than himself; wants to rule his peers	Tends to pick the flashy Hollywood type	Looks up to those with quiet but witty ways	Picks people who stand for something they find meaningful
Positive Experiences	Enjoys controlling, managing, accomplishing	Enjoys performing, being approved of, having fun	Enjoys the flow—isn't disappointed because he doesn't have expectations met	Enjoys creating, perfecting

Self-esteem is fragile and intricate, much like a spiderweb. It is built with much tenacity and care, but it can easily be damaged or torn.

As teachers, we must be wise in how we embrace our students' strengths and weaknesses. We must love our children as God made them. We must communicate that love with our touch, talk, and time. We must be good stewards of what God has given us. We must cherish our children as God has created them, and then in that cherishing love, challenge them to be all they can be.

We should also realize the painful circumstances our children endure day after day. They may take classes in which they feel their performance is lousy. Perhaps they are auditory learners and all of their teachers are visually oriented. Maybe they are somewhat different and get teased mercilessly. Childhood can be a painful, lonely time.

Our job, however, is not to remove children from painful circumstances. Instead, we should help them see God at work even in suffering. I believe that the greatest of God's servants endured tremendous suffering at some time in their lives. It is the fire that perfects. Show me a person who greased through childhood easily because of sports ability or attractiveness, and I'll show you an adult who may struggle greatly. Show me the childhood nerd, and I'll show you an adult who is likely to be sensitive, caring, and wise. Why? Because finding a way to grow through painful experiences creates character.

A teacher who thinks the best way to demonstrate love is to rescue her students from the inevitable pain of life may inadvertently remove her students' best chances for growth in terms of developing a godly character.

Top 10 Self-Esteem Builders

We all want our students to develop positive self-esteem. What can we do to best facilitate this?

1. Love your students unconditionally. Make sure they know it.
2. Talk to your students and help them understand who they are and how they fit into the kingdom.
3. Listen to your students' fears and worries, joys and triumphs, and be there for them.
4. Provide a variety of experiences so your students will create compensating behaviors instead of defenses to protect them from pain.
5. Help your students to identify and articulate their strengths and weaknesses.
6. Make sure your students feel a significant part of your class, know their position in Christ, feel the power of succeeding at who they are, know the love of people, and experience the pleasure of a life yielded to Christ.
7. Help your students to see the gain in pain, the character of the cross, and the true joy of knowing Jesus. With Jesus at the helm of your students' lives, no storm can be too great; no weight can sink their ship. Jesus is the only way to find peace amidst a storm. Help them to live the Lord's way.
8. Help children to see the gifts that God has given them, and show them how to use their gifts for God. For example: a spirit of joy, a patient heart, helpful hands, the gift of mercy, etc.
9. Guide your students into seeing that life is not about their rights but about doing what is right. Provide a strong moral compass for them in the midst of life's storms.
10. Tell your students that the stages of life they are in are only temporary—they won't last forever. Remind them that you will walk the journey with them.

Building Healthy Self Esteem

Fill in the spaces below as you review how to help your students build healthy self-esteem.

I. _____ Self-Esteem

a. Define positive self-esteem:

b. List three behaviors a child with positive self-esteem will exhibit.

c. A teacher brings into the classroom her own _____ , gifts, learning style, and _____ .

II. _____ and Self-Esteem

a. Dorothy Briggs states that children see themselves through two mirrors, what are they?
  1.

  2.

b. Teachers often become the mirrors through which students see themselves. Our verbal and nonverbal _____ become the grid through which children filter their understanding of themselves.

c. Dorothy Briggs writes, "Children rarely question our expectations; instead, they question their personal _____ ."

III. Priceless, not _____

a. Dr. James Dobson states that society has two criteria for measuring self-worth. What are they?

b. What are three things you can do to help children see themselves as priceless?
  1. _____ for and with each child

  2. See each child as the _____ God created him to be and teach him in that way.

  3. _____ , touch, and _____ each child each day.

c. When children do not find approval and acceptance in the eyes of parents or teachers, they often build _____ to ease the pain.

IV. _____ and Self-Esteem

a. List the five basic needs children (and adults) must have met in order to feel good about themselves.

b. What can teachers do to help in meeting these needs in the lives of the students they teach?

c. Review the chart on page 163 to better understand how these needs manifest in each unique personality.

Cherishing and Challenging Children to Develop Responsibility

A Teacher with HEART finds ways to build up responsible workers for the kingdom.

Scripture: "Even a child is known by his actions, by whether his conduct is pure and right" (Proverbs 20:11).

Teaching Objective: To provide ways to train children in developing responsibility and to equip them as effective workers for the kingdom.

Classrooms as Communities

> A classroom, like a community, requires everyone using his gifts for it to function efficiently.

Learning from the Past

I love to read history to relax. I often find myself reflecting. *How did they do it? How did teachers teach after they brought in the wood to build the fire? How did people sit on benches in cold churches when my back hurts sitting on my cushy pew in my heated and air-conditioned building? And how did moms raise 15 children in a log cabin without a TV or VCR or asprin? Whew!* I praise God every day that He allowed me to live now instead of in the past. Yet I am also the one who laments about the decadence of our times, how lazy and disrespectful children can be, and why things aren't the way they used to be.

Let us learn from our forefathers and allow what we learn to impact our generation. Let us bring respect and responsibility into our churches, homes, and schools. Responsible children become responsible by being given things to be responsible for. Children learn to be respectful by seeing others model respect and expecting respect in return.

A classroom can be compared to a community. It requires everyone using his gifts to make it function efficiently. A teacher with HEART realizes that the way we teach children to be responsible is to give them opportunities to demonstrate responsibility. Remember, children are not born knowing how to do a task. They must be trained in the steps. As they master skills, we bring more tasks into the process. A word to the wise: start when they are young! Children *want* to help when they are young. If you say "Well, I'll do it for them; they are too young. I will wait until they are older to let them try this." Yikes! You'll miss a glorious opportunity. The following are examples of things young children are able to do for themselves:

- Bringing their Bibles to church/school
- Pushing in their chairs
- Cleaning up after themselves
- Centers: finishing one thing before they begin another
- Giving their offerings
- Remembering to complete their work
- Praying for one another, and finding ways to serve others

Developing Responsibility in Children

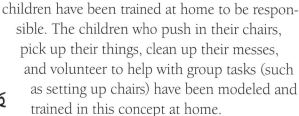

Classroom Activities That Develop Responsibility

There is no big secret as to how to develop responsibility in children. Give them things and tasks to be responsible for in the classroom. As a teacher you can quickly tell which children have been trained at home to be responsible. The children who push in their chairs, pick up their things, clean up their messes, and volunteer to help with group tasks (such as setting up chairs) have been modeled and trained in this concept at home.

As teachers who want to shape hearts, it is important that we train our students to have a servant's heart. Meanwhile, it is wise to train students in practical skills that encourage and empower them to want to be good helpers and to be responsible. Children aren't born knowing how to be responsible, they must be taught. This takes time and patience, but it is an investment that reaps rich dividends. All three of my own children are grown adults. Each have a strong work ethic, and I believe that this is a result of them being trained in how to be responsible at a young age. However, it's never too late to start!

In the classroom a teacher can take the tasks that need to be done and make a chart. Each week after the opening time, the teacher will change who does which chore. The chores are listed and the names of the children are laminated and attached to the chart with self-grip fasteners or reusable adhesive, to make changing the names easier. It helps children feel a part of the classroom to see their names on the chart.

With children up to grade 3, I keep a "mighty magnifying glass" in the classroom. (It is a large wooden frame with a plexiglass magnifying glass inside, which can be purchased for about $10.00 in most stores. They are impressive looking and children love to hold them.) After students have cleaned up the centers, I go around and inspect them with my "mighty magnifying glass" to see if they have been cleaned up properly. After the children learn what you consider to be clean, you can allow them to go and inspect the centers themselves. This cultivates a responsible spirit and involves the entire class in desiring each area to pass inspection. Most children want to hold the "mighty magnifying glass" and will help clean up in the hopes of being able to hold the magnifying glass and complete the inspections.

Our Classroom Helpers

Task	Child's Name
Collect supplies	Ashley
Door holder	Mei Li
Erase the board	Patrick
Lead prayer	Rachel
Line leader	Ty
Pass out supplies	Siena
Read Scripture	Kenan
Wash tables	Victoria

Here are a few other ideas for how to develop responsibility in the children you teach:

- Provide time for children to complete their tasks.
- Rotate jobs each week so that students complete different tasks and learn to master each task by the end of the year.
- Praise their attitude, their abilities, and their accomplishments: "I am so proud of how you persevered on this task."
- Think of what needs to be done in your classroom. If you use centers to encourage hands-on learning and active participation, you will have many tasks. As you add an activity to your classroom, first explain it. Review with your students why it is there, what they can do with it, where it goes, and how to clean it up properly.
- Bible Learning Centers: One of the most effective ways to help children learn to actively use God's Word is through Bible learning centers. Christlike qualities develop and grow as we focus our students' energy in a positive learning environment. Teachers usually think of centers as places that require a budget for supplying many materials. They may regard the concept as impossible due to lack of space and finances. I want to encourage you to think about what a center really is.

What Is A Learning Center?

Here are some answers to the basic questions about learning centers:

- **Who?** All children can benefit from learning centers. Learning centers can be set up purposefully to meet the individual needs of learners as they progress at their own pace.
- **What?** A learning center is a learning activity designed to accomplish specific objectives and to help the learner be more involved.
- **When?** Use learning centers for part of the teaching hour. Or, since children often start arriving early, have a few learning centers ready to make those early minutes count for God. Centers are also an excellent way to end the session as children wait for the closing signal.
- **Where?** Learning centers can be adapted to almost any space or teaching environment. They can be set up in designated areas of the classroom, on part of a shelf, or in a box.
- **Why?** Students learn by interacting and teaching themselves through their experiences. Use the centers to emphasize a

Learning centers are designed to accomplish specific objectives and increase student involvement.

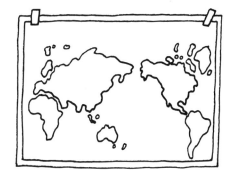

particular point or goal by giving the children opportunities to look at related books, observe items, and work with their hands.

- **How?** As you prepare your lesson, ask yourself: "What activities can I use to reinforce my objective?" Think through the physical logistics of your classroom. Where could you place centers of learning? Here are some suggestions for learning centers in a church setting:

  - Bible maps
  - Bible puzzles
  - Books
  - Crafts
  - Drama
  - Gospel
  - Missions
  - Music
  - Nature
  - Worship

  Here are some suggestions for learning centers in a school setting:

  - Creative corner
  - Maps
  - Math
  - Reading
  - Science

It is important to introduce learning centers slowly, and show the children how to be responsible in caring for each one. Start with only a few and make sure the students understand their purpose and how to leave them orderly for the next student. As students demonstrate proper care for the learning centers, you can add new ones. They will hardly be able to wait to see what comes next!

I try to add a new learning center each week, which means I remove some as well. I had a boy who didn't seem interested in the learning centers until I invited him to show a new child around the classroom. He suddenly came alive as he began to explain everything to the new student. His rhetoric made me realize he had been interested after all!

One way to use learning centers is to designate a certain number of children to work at each center. If a learning center is full (usually no more than one to three children), a child must select another learning center. He may not run from center to center. Part of his training involves him learning to spend a quality amount of time on each activity. Children need to pause, reflect, ponder, and create.

You may choose to rotate the children every 10 minutes. If so, try keeping a chart to ensure that everyone gets a turn at each learning center.

Adapting Your Learning Centers to Lesson Themes

You may choose to leave your learning centers set up in a general way all the time. For some lessons you can add items that relate the specific truth taught that day. Here are some examples of how you might try this:

- **Craft Center**

  Have a white paper cross mounted on a blue sheet of construction paper for each child. The student may confess some of his sins by writing them on his white cross with a red pencil. Then tape a piece of red cellophane over the cross and the sins are no longer visible. This is a reminder that when we confess our sins to God they are forgiven and forgotten because of the blood of Christ (1 John 1:9).

- **Gospel Center**

  Provide a Wordless Book, a Gospel Glove, and other objects that depict the gospel. Another favorite is to provide open cubes in Wordless Book colors that fit inside of each other. As the red cube goes over the dark one, it represents the blood of Jesus completely covering our sins. The white cube over the red one reminds us that we are cleansed from all unrighteousness. The students can look up corresponding verses in the Bible.

  Child Evangelism Fellowship, in Warrenton, Missouri, has excellent resources that present the gospel in color-coded consistency. (See the bibliography at the end of this book for information on how to contact CEF.) Once a child learns the symbolism of the colors, she can use a Wordless Book, which has the colors but no words, and the Gospel Glove, which has the colors on each finger. The color coding is this:

  > **Gold:** Heaven
  >
  > **Black:** Sin (Don't say black but dark because we don't want children to equate black with being bad, from a multicultural standpoint.)
  >
  > **Red:** Blood of Jesus
  >
  > **White:** Our sins are washed clean (Don't say white but clean, so that children do not perceive white as good and black as bad.)
  >
  > **Green:** Growing in Jesus through prayer, worship, going to church, and Bible study.

  Children love the repetition and quickly learn the symbolism. As they grow, children develop, learning additional doctrine and Scripture. The items also grow with the children in their spiritual development and level of understanding. These materials also give children the tools to share the gospel with others as well. Children love these items!

- **Worship Center**

    Place a colorful cloth on a small table and add fresh flowers or a fruit bowl. Place a Bible lying open to a worshipful Psalm. Ask the children how the items can help them worship God. Have them read the Psalm and find ways to worship, direct them to write a worship song to a familiar tune, or take time to say an "I love You" prayer to God.

    If the lesson is on sin and the power of God's forgiveness, you might bring that truth into your worship center in the following ways: Place a list of Bible verses about sin and God's forgiveness on a scroll poster above the worship center. The students can look up the verses and write, on a small scroll provided for each one to take home, two or three of them they would like to remember.

    Another idea is to place a teddybear in the corner. Use the analogy that we all like to snuggle a teddybear. But if it were a real bear, it would hurt us. Sometimes we have our favorite sins, and we get so comfortable with them we don't want to let them go—but we must confess them and stop sinning. Because sin is like a real bear. It will hurt us.

    Children relate to this concept, and the teddy bear serves as a reminder that we must not get comfortable with our sins. Encourage children to ask God to help them to want to let go of a sin in their lives.

    In each of these different learning centers, there are objects for the children to touch and interact with that have spiritual symbolism. Young children are concrete learners and as they are developing abstract concepts, it is wise to have objects that are a part of their world in which to bridge their thinking into spiritual understanding.

Joy in Learning

Children are happier when they are actively involved in the learning process. There is joy when we learn in the way God intended for us to learn, based upon our God-given learning styles.

I once was asked to teach a class that had the reputation of being hard to manage. I quickly saw the reason why these children appeared out of control. They were sitting too long! We began to set up learning centers. The children became focused on accomplishing the activities and the discipline problems went away. One of the children told her parents, "As soon as we did the centers, all the children became good. I guess children need to move to be good." Directed, purposeful activities help children to be their best!

Small Group Discussion: Responsibility In the Classroom

Discuss the following questions to evaluate the responsibility level of the children you teach:

1. List some tasks that your students could help with on a weekly basis.

2. List some of the children in your class who already exhibit responsibility. How do they show this?

3. Why is training your students to be responsible important?

4. What are some ways you can make responsibility-building tasks more enjoyable for the students?

5. What are some areas you would like to see your students grow in over the coming year as they learn to be responsible? What would a responsible student look like at the end of the year? How would he behave?

6. Evaluate your learning centers (if you use them in your classroom). Are they applicable to what you are trying to teach? Are they current? If not, what needs to be changed or updated?

7. If you do not use learning centers, list some kinds of learning centers you could incorporate that would support your classroom goals.

Developing Responsibility

Answer the following questions as you consider how you can incorporate the development of responsibility into your classroom.

1. Children used to learn skills such as cooking, cleaning, etc. at home from working with their parents. What has happened to this lost art in so many families? What can we, as teachers with HEART, do to make up for this void in our culture?

2. Make a drawing of your classroom on a separate sheet of paper. Show how you can add a few learning centers into your space within the confines of your room.

3. What is it about teaching with learning centers that attracts you? What scares you? Develop a prayerful, proactive plan to begin implementing learning centers into your teaching.

4. Fill in the classroom activities that develop responsibility below:
- Use _____ charts.
- Provide adequate _____ for children to complete their tasks.
- Rotate jobs each _____ .
- Praise _____ , abilities, and accomplishments.
- _____ new activities.
- Implement _____ _____ centers.

5. Fill in the following information describing learning centers:
- Who:

- What:

- When:

- Where:

- Why:

- How:

Cherishing and Challenging Children to Make Meaningful Memories

A Teacher with HEART realizes the need to build meaningful traditions of faith.

Scripture: "I will utter hidden things, things from of old—what we have heard and known, what our fathers have told us. We will not hide them from their children; we will tell the next generation the praiseworthy deeds of the Lord" Psalm 78:2-4.

Teaching Objective: To provide a wealth of traditions of our faith for the children we teach.

> We could see that within each tradition, Christ became the ultimate fulfillment and embodiment of truth.

Learning from the Past

During my ministry to children at Grace Bible Church, I planned the usual summer Vacation Bible School program. Each year I would research the different programs and select the one that I felt best met the needs of our church. As time went on, I began to see that the VBS program, which was originally meant to be an outreach program, had now become, in some respects, the local neighborhood babysitting service. We actively sought ways to bring in children from all around the metroplex, especially the inner city. Each year, I prayed to find ways . . .

In my journey to find more ways to enhance our summer ministry programs, I began to study the Jewish festivals. This became a life-changing experience for me. I was deeply impacted by several things I learned but especially by the wealth of the Jewish traditions and how they used the family unit to pass on the heritage of their faith.

As a church, we began to study the Old Testament in a way we had never studied it. As we communicated what we were doing, I had an army of church volunteers rise up to serve. We decided to make it a 12-week church-wide experience, as well as the focus of our regular weekly study. The entire church campus began to reflect the appearance of Bible times. The tents went up and our 12 elders became the 12 tribal leaders. The women and children began to grow the herbs that would be needed. The older men and children began to build items needed. The entire congregation was studying the wealth of teaching of these Old Testament traditions.

As believers we could see that within each tradition, Christ became the ultimate fulfillment and embodiment of truth. We became passionate to reach out to our Jewish community.

The next summer we went on to study more traditions, and then we began to study the tabernacle in depth. "Let's build one, true to biblical standards!" We were off on another journey.

As the neighbors began to see this tabernacle being constructed at a very visible intersection in Dallas, our Jewish neighbors began to come by to see what in the world we were doing. What a way to reach out to them! We were speaking the same language. The faithful Dallas Theological Seminary professors who taught at our church began to study the tabernacle more closely, brought their colleagues, and soon everyone was involved. *The Dallas Morning News* did a full feature on it, complete with many photographs.

The most important aspect of our three-year study is that we, as a church, began to realize that we did not know very much about our heritage. This created a hunger to learn. It also made us real-

> **We grew as a church because we worked together as a family.**

ize that as Christians, we needed to be more effective in building meaningful traditions with our children. Finally, we saw how much we grew as a church because we worked together as a family. Now, where do we go from here?

Gary Swindell is an elder at Grace Bible Church in Dallas. He began an annual tradition, which has continued to grow over the years. He calls it "Experience the Joys of Christmas." Each year our church is transformed into the different scenes surrounding the birth of Christ. The community is invited to join us as we journey through each aspect of the Christmas story.

As my children grew in this tradition, and then began to be involved as participants, this celebration started to have more meaning for us. As we sat in the courtyard and watched the shepherds suddenly see the sky filled with angels singing (that part due to technology), we stepped back into that time period. We could truly sense how profound it was that the angels came to announce the Messiah's coming. From the shepherd, to the manger, to the wise men, we were experiencing the story of the birth of Christ. We never tired of it.

Many churches do the same with the resurrection story. I applaud the passing along of these traditions of our faith in a most experiential way.

We live in a very transient culture. People don't put down roots like they used to, and the extended family is rarely living in one community. With the message of the media, children learn about the Bible through videos, DVDs, tapes and CD's. But it is all two-dimensional learning. Research shows us that this kind of learning does not develop brain patterns in young minds. Children need the rich language of real human beings—active, hands-on, experiential learning in order to remember it, retain it, and retrieve it.

As teachers with HEART, let us take on this crusade for Christ, as we create meaningful memories and rich traditions of our faith for our students.

The Medieval Trivium

Let us take a brief departure to look at a very old model of learning known as the Medieval Trivium. (For an explanation of the Medieval Trivium model go to www.legacyca.com.) In this model we see once again that all truth is God's truth. The Medieval Trivium has three stages of learning. Let's examine them and see how they apply to the passing along of the traditions of our faith.

- Grammar stage (ages 2–11):

    This is a time in which children are eager to learn the stories of our faith. They want to know more and more. Frankly, I am of the conviction that as teachers with HEART who teach using curriculum with HEART (see Chapter 15), this is a critical time to teach the Bible fully as children grow into grades 4–6.

- Logic or Dialectic Stage (ages 12–16):

    This is a time when our students want to debate, dialogue, and dispute everything they have been taught. The child who was hungry for more information in the grammar stage now wants to argue it to death in the logic stage. I am absolutely convinced that this is the stage where we make it or lose it with our children. This is their time to wrap their arms around the information they have been taught and question it, in order to take ownership of it. If we shut them down, we may see them check out of the church and walk away from their faith. But if we are there for them, listen to their questions, and let them debate, dialogue, and dispute in a respectful way, then we can prepare them for the next stage in which they are ready to pass along the wealth of their faith in Jesus Christ.

- Rhetoric Stage (ages 16+):

    This is the stage in which students can take what they learned in the grammar stage, questioned in the logic/dialectic stage, and can now articulate it in a meaningful way in the rhetoric stage.

    With the Medieval Trivium in mind, let us journey through a calendar year and see what we can do on an annual basis to grow traditions of faith in the children we teach in order to build a community of faith.

Meaningful Memories Through the Year

Each teacher needs to come up with special seasonal activities that suit each child she teaches. The very act of planning these events becomes a meaningful memory. Here are a few of the things we have tried, which may work for your classroom.

January

- On New Year's Eve or New Year's Day, reflect on the many ways that the Lord has blessed you during the past year. Write out goals and prayer requests for the New Year. As a class make a list of fun things that you would like to do in the New Year.
- Snow Day parties are also fun. If possible, play outside with the children and then come in and make cookies and drink hot apple cider in front of a warm fire. These create a warm sense of family, fun, and belonging. We have to remember that many of the children we teach have not had these kinds of experiences. These create a strong sense of bonding, which they do not forget.

February

- Make a Love Tree with Bible verses that talk about love written on paper hearts. Hang the hearts as leaves on the tree.
- Make homemade bread, kneaded with your love, for people who may need a little special love. Put a love message on a loaf and deliver it from the students in your class. Children love to make bread and this could become an ongoing ministry. I think freshly baked bread is one of the nicest ways to say I love you.
- Other ideas include making Valentine cookies, making meals for shut-ins, or making handmade cards for people who don't normally receive a Valentine.

March and April

- Celebrate spring. Relate the new life all around you to the new life that we have in Jesus.
- Celebrate March "coming in like a lion or a lamb." What symbolism in the Bible do we have about the Lamb? Who did the lion in *The Lion, the Witch, and the Wardrobe* represent? Discuss it. Read the book again.
- Celebrate Resurrection Sunday. Discuss why we celebrate the resurrection of Jesus at different times each year.

As Christians, celebrating the resurrection of Jesus Christ should be the most important event of the year. It is because of this event that we are Christians. It is worth taking lots of time to celebrate this most sacred of days. Select activities that take a longer time to complete so that the meaning of the day is heightened.

- Make Holy Week Baskets with your students. Select or make items to go into the baskets that represent Holy Week. Such items could include: a palm branch to represent the Triumphal Entry, a small paper towel to represent Jesus washing the disciples' feet, a small communion cup and unleavened bread to represent the Last Supper, a scroll made with two craft sticks and a piece of paper on which your students have written their favorite Gospel verse, a cross made from craft sticks, a piece of black felt to show the world turning dark when Jesus died, grass as a symbol of new life in Jesus, a shroud cloth, a rock to represent the stone over the tomb. Let your students think of additional items.

- Make or purchase Resurrection Eggs. I had been teaching how to make Holy Week Baskets to teachers around the country for over 20 years. Imagine my surprise when I walked into a Christian store and saw Resurrection Eggs! After a twinge of pride, I remembered that all truth is God's truth. I also spiritually chastised myself because I realized that even though I had published this idea 20 years earlier, I certainly had no copyright ownership of the Bible! What could be more profound than children learning even more hands-on techniques about teaching the Bible? Look for Resurrection Eggs at your local Christian bookstore.

- Take "A Walk to the Cross." I stumble as I share this tradition because I cannot name the original source. True to form, I loaned out the book and now cannot find it anywhere. So author, please forgive. I never capitalized on your wonderful lesson but used it per your instruction to teach children and adults. The lesson begins with Old Testament prophecies and moves through the events of Holy Week, to the cross, and ends with the open tomb. Ten various destinations offer opportunities to reflect on an event leading up to the death of Christ. Children can visit a tree to remember when the first sin took place, see and hold a perfume bottle to remember Jesus' being anointed by Mary, or hold a crown of thorns to remember the suffering Jesus experienced.

- Make a Resurrection Shadow Box. Take a shoebox and add something each day (or week) that depicts part of the resurrection message. Three days prior to celebrating the resurrection of Jesus, put the lid on the box and don't add anything. On the day you celebrate the resurrection, add something special to represent the fact that Jesus is alive, and put in a tiny window for your students to peek through. See if the children can find the special item.
- Learn songs that focus on the resurrection and new life in Christ. Even preschoolers will like to try singing these songs.
- You could also make tiny baskets of the following colored jellybeans and include the following poem:
    RED is for the blood He gave.
    GREEN is for the grass He made.
    YELLOW is for the sun so bright.
    BLACK is for the dark of night.
    BLUE is for the sky He made.
    WHITE is for the grace He gave.
    PURPLE is for His hours of sorrow.
    PINK is for our new tomorrow.
    A bag full of jellybeans colorful and sweet,
    Are a prayer, a promise, and a child's treat.
    May the risen Lord bless you,
    Today and always.
Distribute the baskets to unsaved friends. (You may want to add a tract.)

May

- Celebrate Mother's Day. Also remember other women who have helped care for children at church or home, who may not be mothers themselves. Give them a card and flowers. They too play a loving, vital role in many children's lives and may be feeling lonely on this day.

June

- Celebrate Father's Day! Researchers have often stated that our relationship with our Heavenly Father is often formed by our relationship with our earthly father. On this day we need to be sensitive that some children do not have a loving relationship with their earthly father. We can teach them that our Heavenly Father always loves and cares for us. He is there for us no matter how old we are and all we need to do is pray to Him, and He will be there for us.

- You could also research ways for your students to serve during Vacation Bible School.

July

- Set aside a day for fun, including things your students WANT to do instead of planning it all out for them. In the Old Testament, and even still today in Jewish traditions, children are involved in many aspects of preparation. This builds a sense of tradition and will equip them for passing their own traditions along to their children when they are parents.

August

- Time for back to school! Pray about the upcoming year and what you would like to see from this year of learning together.

September

- Set up a prayer tree together. (See Chapter 14.)
- Celebrate the great heritage our children have in their grandparents. In Bible times the traditions were passed on from one generation to another through stories and experiences of everyday life. Today children often visit their grandparents only for fun times. Encourage children to ask their grandparents the following questions about their lives: What was school was like for them? Did they go to church? How did they come to know Jesus?

October

- Fall fun may include taking wonderful walks to collect leaves. Iron them in wax paper and hang them on the windows. There is a rhythm in the year, and the four seasons bring a sense of security in their predictability. Unless a child lives in a tropical climate that does not have a clear distinction between the seasons, most places have a time in which the leaves turn and fall. As these times come, we can ask "Do you remember something from last fall? Was there a prayer request that you had that you can see how God has answered?" Seasons and holidays can become time markers to show God's faithfulness.

- Have a Let Your Light Shine for Jesus party. Carve pumpkins with friendly faces, and put candles inside to represent letting our light shine for Jesus in a dark and sinful world. Find Scripture verses about the light of God. Make pumpkin bread, roast pumpkin seeds, and have a pumpkin-decorating contest. Make sure each child gets a prize for something unique about his pumpkin. Sing songs such as "This Little Light of Mine." Talk about ways to be a light for Jesus in the world. Distribute tracts. Present the gospel.

- Have a Fall Festival! It takes lots of planning and work to make a successful Fall Festival. You can tie it in with many of the Jewish festivals, which were times to celebrate and commemorate one's walk with the Lord.

November

- Talk to your students about what it means to have an attitude of gratitude. It's great to have a grateful heart. Let's train our children in this attitude while they are young.
- Make "I Am Thankful for You" cards for those people who often are forgotten.

December

Try to divert some of the attention from receiving and focus on giving. This is certainly easier said than done in our consumer-minded world. Here are a few suggestions:

- Adopt a needy family.
- Participate in the Angel Tree program. This program is part of Prison Fellowship, Chuck Colson's prison ministry. (Information is available in Christian bookstores.)
- Give baskets of food to needy families.

  Talk with your students, and ask: "What do you think would be a good thing to give to this person or to this organization?" Help them begin to think as givers. Build on this attitude.

- Advent is one of my favorite traditions because it is quiet and pretty. As you light the candles of an Advent wreath in your class, read from Scripture and talk about what it means to live joy, peace, and love. This all builds to the climax when you light the final candle to celebrate the birth of Jesus who is the light of the world.
- Have a birthday party for Jesus, for children who may not know the Lord.

> **Let us counter the culture and cultivate respect in our students!**

A Child's Faith

Joyce Myers is our lower school principal and a dear friend. She has been a minister to children at various churches, as well as a missionary to many places around the world. We are the same age, see things similarly, and have grown children about the same age. We often lament about how certain aspects that are very dear to our hearts seem to be dissipating in our culture. One of these is that children are no longer being taught the hymns of the faith. So at our school, we teach the stories behind the hymns. We want to raise up a remnant of young people who know and appreciate the hymns.

We also are concerned with the lack of manners and respect in our culture. We are very strict about this in our school. We want children to show respect to adults and to know that adults are worthy of respect. So before I leave the chapter on memories, I want to elaborate on this issue of respect. I am absolutely convicted that if we, as believers, do not pass along the art of manners and cultivate a climate for respect, we will lose these vital essentials. There is almost nothing left in our culture upon which to model this critically important concept. Let us counter the culture and cultivate manners in our students! Let this training be a vital part of the memories we leave with our students.

As we have looked at the research by Piaget, Erickson, Kohlberg, and others, we have seen that children learn in different ways at various stages. I am convinced that children at all ages can be taught and expected to demonstrate good manners and respect. Young children do not understand the reason, but they will reflect it back if we model it for them. Start when they are 2 and continue it until they are 20! Every student can respond with "Yes ma'am," "Yes sir," "Please," "Thank you," and "Excuse me," if you require it.

A teacher with HEART will want to create a classroom that cultivates respect. Pray that your classroom will be a source for meaningful memories for each of your students.

The most effective way to reach children is within a community of faith.

In *Will Our Children Have Faith?* John H. Westerhoff, III (2000) discusses another aspect of passing along our faith. He states that faith is best inspired within a faith community. The most effective way to reach children is within a community of faith. When children observe and experience adults modeling faith in their walk with the Lord, the learning occurs in deeper dimensions. Let's look at our churches and schools. Are they environments where faith is alive? Let's provide healthy faith communities where children can be inspired, encouraged, and empowered in their faith.

Making Meaningful Memories

Answer the following questions to explore ways that you can pass on traditions of faith to your students.

1. What traditions do you believe are important to pass on to your students?

2. List three traditions that you would like to begin with the students in your class this year:

1.

2.

3.

3. What value does the extended family and body of Christ have in the faith development of children?

4. What part does practicing good manners play in developing memories in our children? Why is it important? What are some collective goals your church and/or school can set to cultivate this attitude?

5. Brainstorm some traditions you can begin for your church/school for each month that will begin to build in the value of rituals of faith with your students:

January:

February:

March:

April:

May:

June:

July:

August:

September:

October:

November:

December:

The Medieval Trivium

Fill in the following chart to review the Medieval Trivium. Define the three stages of learning in the Trivium model, and state how it impacts your teaching.

Stage:	Ages	Characteristics	How it affects my teaching
Grammar			
Dialectic (or Logic)			
Rhetoric			

Cherishing and Challenging Children with the Power of Prayer

A **Teacher with HEART** trusts in, and relies on, the power of prayer.

Scripture: "Pray in the Spirit on all occasions with all kinds of prayers and requests. With this in mind, be alert and always keep on praying for all the saints" (Ephesians 6:18).

Teaching Objective: To understand the power of prayer, know when children are developmentally ready for different kinds of prayers, and to teach the practical aspects of prayer.

Preparation for Prayer

I was teaching my own children about confession and the peace that you feel when you have confronted a sin and confessed it. We talked about how 1 John 1:9 truly is a Christian's bar of soap. That night as our family prayed, Angela confessed, "Dear God, I am sorry that I took Christopher's car and hid it in my panty drawer." After prayer time Christopher flew out of the room and returned with his car. "So you took my car, huh?"

In complete innocence she responded, "How did you know?"

He promptly retorted, "I just heard you pray about it." "I wasn't talking to you. I was talking to Jesus."

Oh that we may pray so directly to just You, Jesus. Teach us to pray as purely and innocently as a child.

In preparing children for a time of prayer, I tell them the only reason we close our eyes and fold our hands is because this helps us to focus more on God. If we're looking around or fidgeting with something, we are less likely to be focused on the Lord. Does God only answer prayers of children who sit quietly and close their eyes and fold their hands? No. God answers the prayers that we pray from our heart. But quiet hands help the heart to be quieter.

Why do we pray in Jesus' name? Jesus is the road straight to God. When we pray, believing in the power of Jesus, our prayers are carried straight to the throne of Heaven.

> **When we pray, believing in the power of Jesus, our prayers are carried straight to the throne of Heaven.**

Out of the Mouths of Babes

A child's understanding of words is so literal and age appropriate. At our school we recite the Pledge of Allegiance, the Pledge to the Christian Flag, and the Pledge to the Bible each day. One of our teachers was checking to see what the words meant to the pre-K children. Here are the words to the Pledge to the Bible:

"I pledge allegiance to the Bible, God's Holy Word. I will make it a lamp unto my feet, and a light unto my path, and will hide its words in my heart that I might not sin against God."

Here are some of their answers to the question: "What do these words mean to you?"

"About God and the earth."

"Don't sin against God."

"I won't sin against God."

"The Bible is God's Holy Word."

"Hide my words in my heart."

"The Bible verse."

"My heart."

"We never, never, never sin."

"God will keep the words in the Bible."

"It's hard to say."

"God floated to earth."

"It is going to rain and thunder. It is dark outside."

"Put the sin in your heart."

Young children are in a time of absorbing language. They do not have the frame on which to hang the many words they are learning. This illustrates the many different levels of understanding as well as confusion. As teachers we are training in skills for prayer. We are training in righteousness. We are seeking to develop in our students sensitivity to prayer and the things of God. But we must remember that growing a child takes time, but it is certainly better than trying to repair a grownup!

Patterns of Prayer

One of the best patterns we have for prayer is The Lord's Prayer found in Matthew 6. I personally believe in starting to teach this prayer at the kindergarten level. Children can learn the words, but we must be careful to help them truly understand the message. Take time to go through the prayer phrase by phrase with your students. Help each child to articulate it in his own words so that when he prays it, it will have a deeper impact on him.

For the most part I discourage memorized prayers. They do expose children to prayer, at least on some level, and they do present a pattern of praying that may be helpful. However, memorized prayers do not teach a child how to pray sincerely from his own heart.

I think memorized prayers for children ages 2 or 3 are appropriate. At this age they love to learn rhymes. When Angela was 2, her Sunday school teacher taught her a memorized prayer to music. Regardless of where we were, when food was served, she broke into prayerful praise. People who pray, as well as those who don't, are encouraged when they see a 2-year-old spontaneously break into prayer: "And a little child will lead them . . ." (Isaiah 11:6).

I believe that as teachers we should also set a pattern of when we pray and encourage our students to do the same. I have tried to begin the day with the Lord, yet I continue to fail miserably in this area. I set the alarm, but I doze back for five more minutes. When I do get to my prayer chair, I nod off. I have tried everything. This is embarrassing to state publicly.

> **Memorized prayers provide a pattern of praying but do not teach a child how to pray from his own heart.**

Teach your students to pray spontaneously, as the need comes up.

I am a night person. I come alive at about 9:00 P.M. each night and can easily stay up until 1:00 or 2:00 A.M. So my solution is to have my quiet time after everyone else is asleep. First, I write in my journal (including my prayer journal). This process prepares my heart for a quiet, productive, and peaceful time with the Lord. I then read His Word, do my Bible study, and close with prayer time. This works well for me, but I still have the picture in my mind that the true Proverbs 31 woman would greet her Lord each morning in prayer. So I continue to try to work in a regular morning time with God.

I discovered a wonderful little tract called, *Seven Minutes with God* that has helped give my weary body and mind focus in the morning (Foster 1997). This is the structure:

One minute: Prepare your heart (Psalm 143:8).

Four minutes: Read from the Bible.

Two minutes: Prayer organized in the following ways:

    A Adoration (1 Chronicles 29:11)

    C Confession (1 John 1:9)

    T Thanksgiving (Ephesians 5:20)

    S Supplication (Matthew 7:7)

We also need to train our students to pray spontaneously, as the need comes up. When you are driving and see an ambulance or fire truck, pray and encourage your students to pray. Or pray over current events that your students have heard about on the television or radio.

Prayer in the Classroom

Ah, we teach our children so many wonderful things in our classrooms, from Scripture verses and Bible stories to God's truths and how to apply them in our lives. But what about teaching prayer? Teaching prayer? Hold on a minute! No one can teach prayer—you just do it, right? Wrong! We need to teach prayer in our classes as much as we need to teach any of the other wonderful things we work so hard to get through to kids! Prayer isn't an innate activity or one that we're born "just doing" any more than we're born reciting John 3:16 or the Ten Commandments. Yet prayer is perhaps the most overlooked area for instruction in the history of the Christian classroom! Let's explore a little about prayer and why it's essential to provide at least some instruction for kids to understand and grasp the fullness of prayer so they can make it a daily, lifelong habit.

"Lord, teach us to pray, just as John taught his disciples." So begins Luke 11:1 with the disciples' plea to Jesus to instruct them in the way of powerful prayer. Even the disciples knew there must be something more to this intimate time with God than first meets the eye. And just how did Jesus respond? Did He turn them away saying, "Oh, there's no need for that! Just talk to God. It's a natural thing, you know?" No, Jesus took the time to give His disciples a precious lesson about prayer—and us a dear passage of Scripture better known as the Lord's Prayer. Jesus offered us important guidelines for praying to our Heavenly Father and encouraged His disciples to pray in that way. If the disciples recognized the need for prayer and instruction and Jesus provided us a perfect prayer model, why isn't prayer a more studied area in children's Christian education?

Have you ever invited your kids to pray aloud for the class? Chances are you'll see more nervous glances than goodies at a bake sale! Reluctant kids aren't against praying aloud any more than most adults receiving the same invitation. Shyness, insecurity, and lack of words are usually the culprits keeping our kids from the fullness of prayer and the wonderful gift of praying for others in God's presence. . . . When kids have a prayer model and a bit of security, their voices will rise to the Father in beautiful prayers that still all Heaven to hear!

Excerpt from *Disciple Makers* by Susan L. Lingo. Standard Publishing, 2000.

Here are some simple ways to help children learn to pray. As soon as your students want to pray spontaneously on their own, let them. But in the meantime, or if your students feel more secure with a pattern to follow, try these suggestions.

Praying Hand: Using Fingers to Teach Prayer

Age 2

- We fold our hands and as we wiggle our thumbs together, we pray, "Dear God."
- As we wiggle our pointer fingers, we say, "Thank You for my family."
- As we wiggle our middle fingers, we say, "Thank You for Jesus."
- As we wiggle our ring fingers, we say, "Thank You for our church."
- As we wiggle our baby fingers, we say, "In Jesus' name, amen."

Ages 3 and 4

- Thumbs: "I pray for my family." (Thumbs are for those closest to us.)
- Pointer fingers: "Thank You for my friends."
- Middle fingers: "Thank You for Jesus who died on the cross for my sins."
- Ring fingers: "Thank You for the Bible and my church."
- Baby fingers: "Help me to be more like Jesus. In Jesus' name, amen."

At age 4 children can add more specifics for each division. For example, when I pray for my family I pray for Grandma's knee.

Age 5

Introduce the idea of:

- Jesus (thumbs)
- Others (pointer, middle, ring fingers)
- You (baby fingers)

Have children begin praying by first focusing on Jesus. They can thank Him, praise Him, or simply talk to Him. But their focus should be clearly on Jesus. Gently encourage children to focus on Jesus, not their wish list for Jesus. Encourage statements that focus on Jesus such as:

"Thank You, Jesus, for loving me."

"Thank You, Jesus, for dying on the cross for my sins."

"Thank You, Jesus, for helping me today."

"Jesus, You are my best friend."

Discourage prayers that are "I" oriented:

"Jesus, I want a new bike."

"Jesus, please help me pass this test."

Please note: It's OK for a child to ask the Lord to help him. But at this time in his prayer growth we want to help him get to know Jesus.

Use the pointer, middle, and ring fingers to remind children to pray for others. We can help broaden the child's understanding of others to include neighbors, missionaries, teachers, the president, etc.

The *y* in Joy is for *you* (the child). I say, "Now that we have talked to Jesus and prayed for others, we can pray for you. What would you like to pray about for yourself?"

The consistent pattern in all of these prayers is found in putting the child's needs last. Children at this age are in a very egocentric stage of development. We must gradually train in the Christlike attitude of putting others before ourselves.

Here is one more reminder to help stretch praying to a new level. In this exercise the child goes through each of his 10 fingers:

J Jesus

O Others

Y You

F Family

U Use me, Lord (being willing to serve)

L Love (even when it's hard)

A Adore God (praise)

C Confess specific sins

T Thanksgiving

S Supplication

These are simple prayer reminders to help your students grow as prayer warriors. You and your students can make up your own reminders. Praying with the children you teach is really a special time that you can spend together.

Practical Projects

I've mentioned several exercises to help children become more consistent in their prayer lives. Perhaps one of these ideas will help you:

Prayer journals: These are a nice way to keep up with different things that you have prayed for as a class over the year.

Prayer Timelines: I put up an 8 ½ x 11 piece of construction paper for each month of the year. I write prayer requests on different colored index cards and attach them to the construction paper. When a prayer is answered I put a star on the prayer request. You can periodically draw your students' attention to the prayer timeline and reflect on how faithful God is in answering prayers. This becomes a sort of classroom Hebrews 11 to show God's faithfulness.

Prayer Trees: Draw the outline of a tree on a bulletin board or some easy to reach place. Cut out shapes for your tree that change each month. For example:

> January: snowflakes
> February: hearts
> March: shamrocks
> April: lilies
> May: apple blossoms
> September: apples
> October: orange leaves
> November: tan leaves
> December: lights

These shapes don't have to be authentic, botanical items. They can be symbols that represent a holiday or month.

Either you or your students should write prayer requests and put them on the tree. Each day students should all look at the tree. When the prayer requests have been answered, the shapes move to the ground around the bottom of the tree. As the year advances, the top of the tree, as well as the ground under it, becomes a kaleidoscope of prayer requests. Those on top are still unanswered and thus a visible reminder to keep on praying. Those on the bottom serve as a growing reminder of the many prayers God has answered. At the end of each year, gather up all of the answered prayers, put them in a baggie, and place them in boxes that your students can keep. I call these "memory boxes."

> "When kids understand why we pray and what promises God makes to those who pray, a willing and more confident prayer attitude is inevitably born!"
>
> Excerpt from *Disciple Makers* by Susan L. Lingo. Standard Publishing, 2000.

Missions Map: On a world map put a picture of a missionary that you pray for and under it a 3 x 5 card of current prayer requests. Be sure the card can be easily changed. Have a child take a stickpin with yarn wrapped around it that goes from the picture to the place where the missionary is serving. This activity provides a visible reminder to pray for missionaries. It is also a visual reminder that not all missionaries are in Africa (children often think all missionaries go to Africa). And it gives students a sense of geography (when things happen in the news, you can look at the map to see where the events took place).

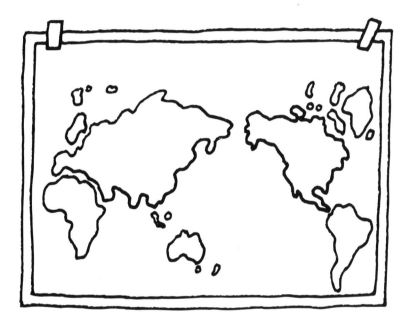

Praying for Fruit

Pray for your students to exhibit the fruit of the Spirit. Select a key Bible verse to use as a prayer guide. The fruit of the Spirit (Galatians 5:22, 23) and other key verses to use are listed below.

Love

Pray for your students to love as God loves. "Live a life of love, just as Christ loved us and gave himself up for us" (Ephesians 5:2).

"Dear friends, let us love one another, for love comes from God. Everyone who loves has been born of God and knows God" (1 John 4:7).

"God is love. Whoever lives in love lives in God, and God lives in him" (1 John 4:16).

"There is no fear in love. But perfect love drives out fear" (1 John 4:18).

Joy

Pray for your students to experience the joy of the Lord when you pray this verse for them: "The joy of the Lord is your strength" (Nehemiah 8:10).

Peace

Pray for the children to know peace. "And the peace of God, which transcends all understanding, will guard your hearts and your minds in Christ Jesus" (Philippians 4:7).

"Peace I leave with you; my peace I give you. I do not give to you as the world gives. Do not let your hearts be troubled and do not be afraid" (John 14:27).

"Turn from evil and do good; seek peace and pursue it" (Psalm 34:14).

"Now may the Lord of peace himself give you peace at all times and in every way. The Lord be with all of you" (2 Thessalonians 3:16).

Patience

Pray for the children you teach to be patient in the power and strength of the Holy Spirit. "You too, be patient and stand firm" (James 5:8).

"Strengthened with all power according to his glorious might so that you may have great endurance and patience" (Colossians 1:11).

"Blessed is the man who perseveres under trial, because when he has stood the test, he will receive the crown of life that God has promised to those who love Him" (James 1:12).

Kindness

Pray for your students to exhibit kindness and compassion toward others. "Be kind and compassionate to one another, forgiving each other, just as in Christ God forgave you" (Ephesians 4:32).

Goodness

Pray for the children you teach to exhibit the goodness that comes from a renewed spirit in Jesus Christ. "With this in mind, we constantly pray for you, that our God may count you worthy of his calling, and that by his power he may fulfill every good purpose of yours and every act prompted by your faith" (2 Thessalonians 1:11).

"For we are God's workmanship, created in Christ Jesus to do good works, which God prepared in advance for us to do" (Ephesians 2:10).

Faithfulness

First and foremost, pray for the children you teach to come to faith in Jesus Christ as their Lord and Savior. "For it is by grace you have been saved, through faith—and this not from yourselves, it is the gift of God" (Ephesians 2:8).

Pray that their faith will grow strong in their daily walk with the Lord: "But I have prayed for you . . . that your faith may not fail. And when you have turned back, strengthen your brothers" (Luke 22:32).

"Be on your guard; stand firm in the faith; be men of courage; be strong" (1 Corinthians 16:13).

"Fight the good fight of the faith" (1 Timothy 6:12).

Pray that your students will be ever faithful in service to the living God: "Therefore, since we are receiving a kingdom that cannot be shaken, let us be thankful, and so worship God acceptably with reverence and awe" (Hebrews 12:28).

Gentleness

Pray that your students will "slander no one, . . . be peaceable and considerate, and . . . show true humility toward all men" (Titus 3:2).

Also pray that they will "pursue righteousness, godliness, faith, love, endurance and gentleness" (1 Timothy 6:11).

Pray for them to be the kind of people the following verse describes so beautifully: "Instead, it should be that of your inner self, the unfading beauty of a gentle and quiet spirit, which is of great worth in God's sight" (1 Peter 3:4).

Self-Control

Finally, pray for your students to have the self-control that flows from a spirit-controlled life. "But if you are led by the Spirit, you are not under law. . . . But the fruit of the Spirit is love, joy, peace, patience, kindness, goodness, faithfulness, gentleness, and self-control. Against such things there is no law. . . . Since we live by the Spirit, let us keep in step with the Spirit" (Galatians 5:18, 22, 23, 25).

> First and foremost, pray for the children you teach to come to faith in Jesus Christ as their Lord and Savior.

Pray Without Ceasing

I wanted the children at church and at school to realize that prayer was not confined to a particular place, time, or physical position, such as hands folded or eyes closed. I used 1 Thessalonians 5:17 as the Scripture to encourage them to pray anytime, anywhere, and for any reason. I also wanted them to realize that God may talk to us anytime, anywhere, and for any reason. We may be riding our bikes when we sense the Lord calling us to do something. Does He only call us for the big jobs like being a missionary in Africa, or can He call us for the seemingly little jobs as well, such as helping our neighbor carry in groceries?

My goal was to help train the children to practice the presence of God as a daily habit. I wanted them to talk to their Heavenly Father about all of their needs, to be attuned to listen to His still, quiet voice, and to respond with obedience. Thus, I remind them to "pray without ceasing" (1 Thessalonians 5:17, *King James Version).*

One day as the children were leaving chapel and I was collecting hugs at the door, one little guy said, "I'm sorry I sneezed during your prayer, Mrs. Capehart." I hugged him and assured him that it was no problem because we certainly can't control when those ole sneezes come.

He responded, "But I know you like us to pray without sneezing." Isn't that wonderful? So you may pray and sneeze, but please don't cease praying. May God bless you as you grow in your own prayer life by praying with and for your students.

Prayer Exercises

Complete the following questions and activities to review the prayer exercises mentioned in this chapter.

1. What do you pray for your students? Take a 3 x 5 note card and jot down three things that you want to pray for your students this week. Look back after a few weeks and make a note of answers to these prayers.

2. Pray with your students this week. If this is a new experience for you, pray the Lord's Prayer with them. Slowly begin to pray about other matters with your students.

3. For older students make a Prayer Timeline and see how God has answered prayers during the year.

4. For students in pre-K to grade 5, make a Prayer Tree. See how the lives of the children are transformed by this experience and how their understanding of prayer deepens.

5. Bring in a newspaper once a month and show the students how to pray for others, even if they don't know them. Cut out different stories and glue them on construction paper. Have a student take a story and pray for it all week and the following week share what the Lord taught him through the experience.

The Power of Prayer

Chapter 14: Cherishing and Challenging Children with the Power of Prayer

Praying for Fruit

What fruit of the Spirit would you like to include in your prayers for your students this week? Find a key verse for each category to recite in praying for your students.

Fruit of the Spirit	Prayer Request	Verse
Love		
Joy		
Peace		
Patience		
Kindness		
Goodness		
Faithfulness		
Gentleness		
Self-control		

Cherishing and Challenging Children by Using Curriculum with HEART

A Teacher with HEART understands the importance of finding and using Bible curriculum resources that help students live holy lives and that are easy to teach, age appropriate, relevant to the culture, and true to the Bible.

Scripture: "From infancy you have known the holy Scriptures, which are able to make you wise for salvation through faith in Christ Jesus. All Scripture is God-breathed and is useful for teaching, rebuking, correcting and training in righteousness" (2 Timothy 3:15, 16).

Teaching Objective: To use curriculum resources with HEART.

Holy Lives

Chapter 2 describes a teacher with HEART and stresses the importance of modeling holy lives for our students. "As teachers with HEART we must strive to lead holy lives and to encourage and teach our students to be set apart for the Lord." Our ministry to children is to help them grow up in Christ. Everything we do must help them grow and mature in Christ. And so finding and using curriculum resources that help us accomplish that goal is important to teachers with HEART.

Curriculum that is focused on helping students grow up in Christ includes activities, themes, and methods that help children love, learn, and live God's Word. Bible stories, lesson topics, and issues are chosen and addressed at the appropriate age levels so students learn who God is, what He did, what He wants; who Jesus is, what He did, what He wants; what the church is, what it did and does today, and how the Holy Spirit works in the lives of people to accomplish God's will.

But more than that, when curriculum is focused on helping children live holy lives, it leads teachers and students to think and act on these questions: What has God done for me? What does God want me to do? What did Jesus do for me? What does He want me to do? How can I be involved in what God is doing? How can I let God's Holy Spirit guide my life?

- 1s and 2s:
  We can prepare the youngest learners for a life of holiness by introducing them to God through the community of faith. They begin to understand God's heart through the love and care shown by parents and teachers. Curriculum materials need to support and remind teachers of 1s and 2s that these little hearts are developing attitudes, or first impressions, of God, Jesus, and the church. Lessons should incorporate lots of interesting and multisensory activities to teach simple Bible concepts, and provide opportunities for teachers and children to talk, laugh, and play together. Children need to see how much their teachers love God, and they need to hear their teachers speak in loving tones.

- Preschoolers:
  Preschool children are ready to hear lots of Bible stories. Through stories of Bible people, children learn about God and Jesus. It is not the Bible characters children need to know; it is God and His Son that children are getting to know. They are getting to know what God has done and what He is like, what Jesus did and what He is like, and what God and Jesus have

asked us to do. Curriculum lessons for this age group should provide a variety of opportunities for students to learn through exploration, through their senses, and through action songs and rhymes. Use concrete activities to demonstrate abstract qualities; teach age-appropriate concepts that children can apply to their lives. Model how you are growing up in Christ, because they will want to please you and imitate you.

- Early Elementary
  Early elementary children are in a time of transition. Sometimes they are like preschoolers, and sometimes they are more like older elementary students. Curriculum with HEART will provide learning opportunities that allow beginning readers and writers to have successful experiences in class. Interactive, fresh presentations of Bible stories and truths will help 1st and 2nd graders take another look at what God is like.

- Middle Elementary
  Middle elementary children are moving from *learning to read* to *reading to learn*. They are in the calmest period of their lives in terms of physical growth. Even though they may have heard Bible stories from birth, this is the time when they can put the stories into perspective and attach meaning to what they have heard. Curriculum with HEART will focus on giving these children a framework on which to hang what they will learn the rest of their lives. The curriculum will give these students the what and why according to Scripture—Bible knowledge, Bible skills, godly standards of behavior, moral values, and a biblical worldview that will become the foundation for their commitment to Christ and ongoing growth with Him.

- Preteens
  Preteens are in transition from children's ministry to student ministry. A curriculum that recognizes this will focus on helping these students gain the attitude that Scripture has the answers for every kind of practical problem or issue they will face. Preteens can grow in Christ by understanding the importance of hiding God's Word in their hearts, by deciding to change behavior because of the Word, and by learning to rely on prayer and God's Holy Spirit to change their behavior. Preteens, more than any other age level of children, need to see that God's Word is relevant to their lives.

Easy to Teach

A teacher with HEART has a teachable spirit; she is approachable, open to correction, willing to learn from others, and respectful of others. But what makes Bible curriculum easy to teach? What makes it easy to use? Curriculum with HEART must be:

- Consistent:
  Curriculum must be consistent in quality—solid Bible teaching through stories and activities, through thematic units and topical studies, and through Bible chronology and Bible skills. Each age level needs appropriate learning experiences and interaction with God's Word.

- Structured:
  Curriculum must be structured around an obvious learning process. Lessons must be designed to help teachers see why every step is important and to give teachers the big picture of what the lesson should accomplish. Units of lessons should connect because kids learn over extended periods of time. Activities should be structured to help kids learn by doing and thinking about what they did.

- Flexible:
  Curriculum must be flexible for a variety of learning situations. Is it easily adaptable to large classes? Are the teaching tips helpful? Does it have optional activities? Is there variety? Is it written with the inexperienced teacher in mind? Look for curriculum with the resources you need (music CDs, correlated classroom activities, colorful visuals).

- Well designed:
  Curriculum that is easy to use needs good design. Is it easy to read? Can I quickly find what I need? Are all the parts and pieces there and easily identified? Are the instructions clear? Is everything integrated well so I know how to use everything I have?
  Curriculum that is easy to teach will help the teacher become the guide and facilitator in the classroom. It will help the teacher interact with the students confidently, allowing her to focus on cherishing and challenging each child. It will also provide the age-appropriate tools teachers need to help children grow up in Christ.

Age Appropriate

Curriculum that is truly age appropriate is based on an understanding of how children learn. It provides Bible lessons based on that understanding and includes in every lesson activities and learning experiences for a range of abilities within an age group.

It can target the Bible stories, concepts, and applications that are appropriate for one age level, and then build on those lessons for the next age level. Thus Bible stories and lesson topics are carefully chosen and addressed at the most appropriate time in a child's life.

Bible skills can be integrated when learners are ready to develop those abilities. Curriculum for toddlers can focus on one concept for a whole month while elementary learners dive into Bible chronology because they finally understand the concept of time.

- Toddlers and 2s

  Curriculum that is age appropriate for toddlers and 2s will include simple concepts, simple songs, sensory activities, reality-based learning, and a flexible lesson structure. There will be lots of opportunities for children to explore, discover, and move. Teachers will be guided to sing, play, talk, and repeat activities, giving young ones time to smile, laugh, and wonder.

- Preschoolers

  Preschool Bible curriculum should build on the concepts taught to younger children—adding more Bible stories, integrating pre-reading skills, continuing to include multisensory experiences, incorporating simple group games, offering activities that stimulate imaginations, and guiding the teacher to take time to answer lots of questions.

- Elementary

  Curriculum for early elementary children is developed with the beginning reader and writer in mind. Helpful tips should be given to guide each teacher to adapt activities to meet the needs of the students in her class. Integrating Bible skills and Bible memorization into curriculum doesn't mean students are now expected to sit down and listen, but attention spans do lengthen and middle elementary kids are eager to learn about God and how they fit in His plan. The issues and topics presented to preteens build on the solid foundation laid in the early elementary years, making it possible for teachers to encourage them beyond "right" and "wrong" answers.

What makes curriculum age appropriate? A clear understanding of child development with a targeted approach to learning that accommodates that understanding. Multiple intelligences, learning styles, brain development, current research, differences in the cognitive development of boys and girls—all of these can be incorporated into curriculum that emphasizes age appropriateness.

Relevant to Culture

It can be a challenge for publishers to keep printed curriculum up-to-date and relevant to the culture, but it can be done. Publishers who understand the importance of this characteristic revise, make changes on a consistent schedule, and take advantage of the Internet to keep Bible lessons relevant to what's happening in learners' lives.

Find and use curriculum that will be relevant to the needs of your students. Music, illustrations, and photos that aren't current can detract from student resources and take-home materials. Curriculum that is relevant will take an approach to learning that can be adapted to include cultural illustrations and examples from students' lives. Teaching tips can guide teachers to incorporate life into lessons by finding and adding current trends, methods, information, and terminology that reflect the culture. Curriculum with on-line lesson connections, or curriculum that is only available on-line, has the capability of staying relevant and providing for teachers weekly cultural insight for that week's lesson.

Curriculum with HEART helps teachers guide students to live holy lives in this world of unholiness. Curriculum that is serious about being relevant to culture will help students develop a biblical worldview—the perspective that Scripture addresses every life need they will ever face.

True to the Bible

Scripture is the focus of Christian education. Scripture teaches us what God wants us to know. Scripture hidden in our hearts helps us live holy lives. Scripture is a guide, a light that produces faith when we hear it.

Curriculum that is true to the Bible not only faithfully presents what Scripture says, but it keeps Scripture at the heart of learning. Every lesson gives children the opportunity to interact with Scripture or use a Bible. Every lesson helps children discover what the Bible says, and then make an age-appropriate response. Every lesson helps children learn Bible words, verses, or passages that help them measure their thoughts, words, and actions.

Curriculum with HEART respects the authority of the Bible, is built on the Bible, covers Bible content in age-appropriate ways, engages each learner with the Bible, and develops students' Bible skills.

Curriculum that is true to the Bible helps children learn who God is and what Scripture is about. It helps children demonstrate the ability to do what Scripture says once they know what it says. It helps children learn the importance of hiding God's Word in their hearts. It helps children learn to change behavior because of the Word. It helps children develop the ability and pattern of daily learning from God's Word. It helps children learn from God's Word on their own, so they can do it for the rest of their lives. It leads children to make a commitment to Jesus as Savior and Lord and challenges them to help others do the same.

Curriculum with HEART is focused on helping children live holy lives, transformed by God's Spirit—so it is developed and resourced to be easy to teach, age appropriate, relevant to culture, and true to the Bible.

Curriculum with HEART

Curriculum Evaluation

Theological Considerations

1. Are the materials based on the Scriptures as the major instructional source?
2. Do the materials encourage the learner to commit him/herself to Jesus Christ?
3. Do the materials connect the learner's relationship with Jesus and his/her relationship with other people?
4. Do the materials support, and teach, the major doctrines of the Christian faith?

Substance and Organization

5. Do the lessons include clear, attainable, age-appropriate, objectives that can be measured?
6. Do the lessons contain a four-part process (attention getters, Bible content time, activities, and application)?
7. Do the lessons employ an adequate number of modes (learning styles)?
8. Do the lessons employ some sort of review of past lessons periodically?
9. Do the lessons build on one another as the learners' knowledge increases?
10. Do the lessons include strong "application" suggestions?

Teacher Support

11. Does the material provide the teacher with adequate background information for the scriptural passage?
12. Does the material provide several options for the teacher to choose in teaching the lesson?
13. Does the material provide supplementary teaching aids, such as maps, pictures, overhead projections, audio recordings, etc.?
14. Does the material provide the teacher with evaluation tools such as tests, etc.?
15. Are the lessons time-appropriate for the average class period?
16. Are the lessons written with the inexperienced teacher in mind?
17. Do the lessons contain specific teacher-talk and guidelines for each phase of the lesson?
18. Are the student books easy to use by the teacher?
19. Does the material require an unrealistic amount of teacher preparation?
20. Are the lesson supplies not included in the curriculum listed clearly?
21. Are the extra lesson supplies "common" craft supplies which every church has?
22. Does the curriculum include parent support, such as letters, family activities, etc.?

Excerpt from *Growing a Healthy Children's Ministry* by Steve Alley. Standard Publishing, 2002.

Defining Curriculum with HEART

Fill in the chart below to assess whether your current curriculum meets the standards of being a curriculum with HEART, and if not, what would help it to do so.

Curriculum Characteristic	How does your curriculum achieve these characteristics?	What would give your curriculum more HEART?
Holy Lives (goal of teaching)		
Easy to Teach		
Age Appropriate		
Relevant to Culture		
True to the Bible		

Barna, George. *Transforming Children Into Spiritual Champions: Why Children Should Be Your Church's #1 Priority*. Ventura, CA: Issachar Resources, A Division of Barna Research Group, Ltd., 2003.

Berends, Polly Berrien. *Gently Lead: How to Teach Your Children about God While Finding Out for Yourself*. New York, NY: HarperCollins, 1991.

Bolton, Barbara, Wesley Haystead, and Charles T. Smith. *Everything You Want to Know About Teaching Children*. Ventura, CA: Regal Books, 1987.

Briggs, Dorothy. *Your Child's Self Esteem: The Key to His Life*. Garden City, NY: Doubleday, 1970.

Cavalletti, Sofia. *The Religious Potential of the Child: The Description of an Experience with Children from Ages Three to Six*. trans. Patricia M. Coulter and Julie M. Coulter. New York, NY: Paulist Press, 1983.

Ciona, John R. *Solving Church Education's Ten Toughest Problems*. Wheaton, IL: Victor Books, 1990.

Coleman, Robert E. *The Master Plan of Discipleship*. Old Tappan, NJ: Fleming H. Revell, 1987.

Coles, Robert. *The Moral Life of Children*. Boston, MA: Houghton Mifflin, 1987.

Coles. *The Spiritual Life of Children*. Boston: Houghton Mifflin, 1990.

Costa, A.L. (Ed.) *Developing Minds: A Resource Book for Teaching Thinking*. Alexandria, VA: Association for Supervision and Curriculum Development, 1985.

Covey, Stephen R. *Principle-Centered Leadership*. New York, NY: Summit Books, 1991.

Crabb, Lawrence J., Jr. *Understanding People*. Grand Rapids, MI: Zondervan, 1987.

Dobson, James, and Gary Bauer. *Children at Risk*. Waco, TX: Word, Inc., 1990.

Dobson, James. *Hide or Seek*. Old Tappan, NJ: Fleming Revell, 1974.

Elkind, David. *All Grown Up and No Place to Go: Teenagers in Crisis*. Boulder, CO: Perseus Books Group, 1997.

Elkind. *The Hurried Child: Growing Up Too Fast Too Soon*. Cambridge, NY: Da Capo Press, 1981.

Elkind. *Miseducation: Preschoolers at Risk*. New York, NY: Alfred A. Knopf, 1987.

Erikson, Erik H. *Childhood and Society*. New York, NY: W.W. Norton, 1985.

Fine, Eddie, and Billye Joyce. *Teachers are Made, Not Born*. Cincinnati, OH: Standard Publishing, 1990.

Flynn, Leslie. *Nineteen Gifts of the Spirit*. Wheaton, IL: Victor Books, 1974.

Ford, LeJoy. *Design for Teaching and Training*. Nashville, TN: Broadman Press, 1978.

Foster, Robert D. *Seven Minutes with God: How to Plan a Daily Quiet Time*. Colorado Springs, CO: NavPress, The Navigators, 1997.

Fowler, James W. *Faith Development and Pastoral Care*. Minneapolis, MN: Fortress Press, 1987.

Fowler. *Stages of Faith: The Psychology of Human Development and the Quest for Meaning*. San Francisco: Harper & Row, 1981.

Fowler. "Strength for the Journey: Early Childhood Development in Selfhood and Faith," in *Faith Development in Early Childhood*. ed. Foris A. Blazer, Kansas City, MO: Sheed and Ward, 1989.

Fowler. *Weaving the New Creation: Stages of Faith and the Public Church*. New York, NY: HarperCollins, 1991.

Friedeman, Matt. *The Master Plan of Teaching*. Wheaton, IL: Victor Books, 1990.

Gangel, Kenneth O. *Twenty-Four Ways to Improve Your Teaching*. Wheaton, IL: Victor Books, 1974.

Gangel. *Unwrap Your Spiritual Gifts*. Wheaton, IL: Victor Books, 1984.

Grant, Reg, and John Reed. *Telling Stories to Touch the Heart*. Wheaton, IL: Victor Books, 1990.

Gregory, John Milton. *The Seven Laws of Teaching*. Grand Rapids, MI: Baker Book House, 1981.

Haystead, Wes. *Everything You Want to Know About Teaching Young Children*. Ventura, CA: Regal Books, 1989.

Haystead. *Teaching Your Child About God*. Ventura, CA: Regal Books, 1981.

Hendricks, Howard. *Teaching to Change Lives*. Portland, OR: Multnomah Press, 1987.

Highet, Gilbert. *The Art of Teaching*. New York, NY: Alfred A. Knopf, 1968.

Horne, Herman H. *The Teaching Techniques of Jesus*. Grand Rapids, MI: Dregel, 1974.

Kjos, Berit. *Your Child and the New Age*. Wheaton, IL: Victor Books, 1990.

Kohlberg, Lawrence, "My Personal Search for Universal Morality," in *The Kohlberg Legacy for the Helping Professions*. Lisa Kuhmerder, Birmingham, AL: R.E.P. Books, 1991.

Kohlberg. *The Psychology of Moral Development Essays of Moral Development*. vol. 1, San Francisco: Harper & Row, 1981.

Kohlberg. "Stages and Sequence: The Cognitive Developmental Approach to Socialization," in *Handbook of Socialization Theory and Research*. ed. David A. Goslin, Chicago, IL: Rand McNally, 1969.

Kuhlman, Edward. *The Master Teacher*. Old Tappan, NJ: Fleming H. Revell, 1987.

LeBar, Lois. Education That Is Christian. Old Tappan, NJ: Fleming H. Revell, 1958.

LeBar, Mary. *Children Can Worship*. Wheaton, IL: Victor Books, 1976.

LeFever, Marlene D. *Creative Teaching Methods*. Elgin, IL: David C. Cook, 1985.

Lingo, Susan. *Disciple Makers*. Cincinnati, OH: Standard Publishing, 2000.

Lingo. *Joy Builders*. Cincinnati, OH: Standard Publishing, 2001.

Littauer, Florence. *Raising the Curtain on Children*. Waco, TX: Word, Inc., 1988.

Lopez, Diane D. *Teaching Children: A Curriculum Guide to What Children Need to Know at Each Level Through Grade Six*. Westchester, IL: Crossway Books, 1991.

Lowrie, Roy. *The Teacher's Heart*. Whittier, CA: The Association of Christian Schools International, 1984.

Macaulay, Susan Schaeffer. *For the Children's Sake*. Westchester, IL: Crossway Books, 1984.

Mahedy, William and Janet Bernardi. *A Generation Alone: Xers Making a Place in the World*. Downers Grove, IL: InterVarsity Press, 1994.

Packer, James I. *Deepening in Step With Spirit*. Old Tappan, NJ: Fleming H. Revell, 1984.

Peters, Thomas J., and Robert H. Waterman, Jr. *In Search of Excellence*. New York, NY: Harper and Row, 1982.

Piaget, Jean. *The Moral Judgment of the Child*. New York, NY: The Free Press, 1965.

Piaget, Jean, and Barbel Inhelder. *The Psychology of the Child*. New York, NY: Basic Books, 1969.

Piaget. *Six Psychological Studies*. New York, NY: Vintage Books, 1967.

Plueddemann, James. *Education That is Christian*. Wheaton, IL: Victor Books, 1989.

Reed, James E., and Ronnie Prevose. *A History of Christian Education*. Nashville, TN: Broadman and Holman, 1993.

Richards, Lawrence O. *Children's Ministry*. Grand Rapids, MI: Zondervan Publishing House, 1983.

Richards. *Children's Ministry, Nurturing Faith within the Family of God*. Grand Rapids, MI: Zondervan, 1983.

Robinson, Edward. *The Original Vision: A Study of the Religious Experience of Childhood*. Oxford: The Religious Experience Research Unit, Manchester College, 1977.

Schimmels, Cliff. *I Learned It First in Sunday School*. Wheaton, IL: Victor Books, 1991.

Selig, George, and Alan Arroyo. *Loving Our Difference*. Virginia Beach, VA: CBN Publishing, 1989.

Shafer, Carl. *Excellence in Teaching With the Seven Laws*. Grand Rapids, MI: Baker Book House, 1985.

Stewart Sonja M., and Jerome W. Berryman. *Young Children and Worship.* Louisville, KY: Westminster/John Knox Press, 1989.

Stonehouse, Catherine. *Joining Children on the Spiritual Journey.* Grand Rapids, MI: Baker Books, 1998.

Stonehouse. *Patterns in Moral Development.* Waco, TX: Educational Products Division, 1980.

Temple, Joe. *Know Your Child.* Grand Rapids, MI: Baker Book House, 1974.

Towns, Elmer. *One-Hundred-and-Fifty-Four Steps to Revitalize Your Sunday School.* Wheaton, IL: Victor Books, 1989.

Trent, John and Cindy; Smalley, Gary and Norma. *The Treasure Tree.* Dallas, TX: Word

Voges, Ken. DISC. In His Grace, 3006 Quincannon Lane, Houston, TX 77043. www.INHISGRACEINC.COM

Wagner, C. Peter. *Your Spiritual Gifts Can Help Your Church Grow.* Ventura, CA: Regal Books, 1974.

Webster's Dictionary, 1928, s.v. "Challenging."

Webster's Dictionary, 1928, s.v. "Cherishing."

Westerhoff, III John H. *Will Our Children Have Our Faith?* Toronto, Canada: Morehouse Publishing, 2000.

Williams, Linda VerLee. *Teaching for the Two-Sided Mind.* New York, NY: Simon and Schuster, Inc., 1983.

Willis, Wesley R. *Developing the Teacher in You.* Wheaton, IL: Victor Books, 1990.

Willis. *Make Your Teaching Count.* Wheaton, IL: Victor Books 1985.

Wlodkowski, R.J., and J.H. Jaynes. *Eager to Learn: Helping Children Become Motivated and Love Learning.* San Francisco, CA: Jossey-Bass Publishers, 1990.

Zuck, Roy B. *The Holy Spirit in Your Teaching.* Wheaton, IL: Victor Books, 1995.

BRAIN RESEARCH

Ackermain, S. *Discovering the Brain.* Washington, D.C.: National Academy Press 1992.

Amen, Daniel G., M.D. *Change Your Brain Change Your Life.* New York, NY: Three Rivers Press, 1998.

Armstrong, T. *The Myth of the ADD Child.* New York, NY: Crown, 1995.

Ayers, J. *Sensory Integration and Learning Disorders.* Los Angeles, CA: Western Psychological Services, 1972.

Ayers. *Sensory Integration and Learning Disorders.* Los Angeles, CA: Western Psychological Services, 1991.

Caine, R.N., and G. Caine. *Making Connections: Teaching and the Human Brain.* Menlo Park, CA: Addison-Wesley, 1994.

Calvin, W. *How Brains Think.* New York, NY: Basic Books, 1996.

Gazzaniga, M. *Mind Matters: How Mind and Brain Interact to Create Our Conscious Lives.* Boston, MA: Houghton-Mifflin/MIT Press, 1988.

Gilbert, A.G. *Teaching the Three R's Through Movement Experiences.* New York, NY: Macmillam Publishing, 1977.

Hannaford, C. *Smart Moves.* Arlington, VA: Great Ocean Publishing Co., 1995.

Healy, J. *Endangered Minds: Why Our Children Can't Think.* New York, NY: Simon and Schuster, 1990.

Healy. *Your Child's Growing Mind.* New York, NY: Doubleday, 1994.

Howard, P. *Owner's Manual for the Brain.* Austin, TX: Leornian Press, 1994.

Hutchinson, M. *MegaBrain Power.* New York, NY: Hyperion Books, 1994.

Jensen, Eric. *Brain Compatible Strategies.* San Diego, CA: The Brain Store, Inc., 1997.

Jensen. *Teaching with the Brain in Mind.* Alexandria, VA: Association for Supervision and Curriculum Development, 1998.

Katz, Lawrence C., and Manning Rubin. *Keep Your Brain Alive*. New York, NY: Workman Publishing Company, 1999.

Kearney, P. "Brain Research Shows Importance of Arts in Education," in *The Star Tribune*, p. 19A, August 3, 1996.

Kotulak, R. Inside the Brain. Kansas City, MO: Andrews and McMeel, 1996.

Kovalik, S. *ITI: The Model-Integrated Thematic Instruction*. Kent, WA: Books for Educators, 1994.

LaBerge, D. *Attention Processing*. Cambridge, MA: Harvard University Press, 1995.

Lamb, S.J., and A.H. Gregory. "The Relationship Between Music and Reading in Beginning Readers," in *Educational Psychology,* 13, 2: 19-26, 1993.

Lasley, E. "How the Brain Learns and Remembers," in *BrainWork* 7, 1: 9, 1997.

LeDoux, J. *The Emotional Brain*. New York, NY: Simon and Schuster, 1996.

Michaud, E., and R. Wild. *Boost Your Brain Power*. Emmaus, PA: Rodale Press, 1991.

Thompson, R. *The Brain*. New York, NY: W.H. Freeman Company, 1993.

Turkington, C. *The Brain Encyclopedia*. New York, NY: Facts on File, 1996.

Vincent, J.D. *The Biology of Emotions*. Cambridge, MA: Basil Blackwell, 1990.

CENTERS

Bolton, Barbara J. *How to Do Bible Learning Activities, Grades 1-6*. Ventura CA: Gospel Light Publications, 1982.

Crisci, Elizabeth W. *What Do You Do With Joe? Problem Pupils and Tactful Teachers*. Cincinnati, OH: Standard Publishing, 1981.

Grogg, Evelyn Leavitt. *Bible Lessons for Little People*. Cincinnati, OH: Standard Publishing, 1980.

Klein, Karen. *How to Do Bible Learning Activities, Ages 2-5*. Ventura , CA: Gospel Light Publications, 1982.

Lee, Rachel Gillespie. *Learning Centers for Better Christian Education*. Valley Forge, PA: Judson Press, 1981.

Pratt, David. *Curriculum Design and Development*. New York, NY: Harcourt Brace Jovanovich, Inc., 1980.

Price, Max. *Understanding Today's Children*. Nashville, TN: Convention Press, 1982.

Warren, Ramona. *Preschoolers Can Do Centers*. Elgin, IL: David C. Cook 1991.

CHILD DEVELOPMENT

Ames, Louise Bates, and Sidney Baker, and Frances L. Ilg. *Child Behavior*. New York, NY: Barnes and Noble Books, a division of Harper and Row Publishers, 1981.

Ames, Louise Bates, et al. *Don't Push Your Preschooler*. revised ed. New York, NY: Harper and Row, 1981.

Ames, Louise Bates. *Is Your Child In the Wrong Grade?* Lumberville, PA: Modern Learning Press, 1978.

Barbour, Mary A. *You Can Teach 2's and 3's*. Wheaton, IL: Victor Books, 1989.

Gangel, Elizabeth, and Elisabeth McDaniel. *You Can Reach Families Through Babies*. Wheaton, IL: Victor Books, 1986.

Gesell, Arnold. *The Child From Five to Ten*. revised ed. New York, NY: Harper and Row, 1977.

Ilg, Frances L. *School Readiness: Behavior Tests Used at the Gesell Institute*. New York, NY: Harper and Row, 1978.

LeBar, Mary E., and Betty A. Hey. *You Can Teach 4's and 5's*. Wheaton, IL: Victor Books, 1987.

McDaniel, Elisabeth. *You Can Teach Primaries*. Wheaton, IL: Victor Books, 1987.

DISCIPLINE

Canter, Lee and Associates. *Assertive Discipline: Positive Behavior Management For Today's Schools (Rev. ed)*. Santa Monica, CA: Lee Canter and Associates. 1994.

Capehart, Jody. *Discipline by Design*. Dallas, TX: The Sampson Company, 2004.

Capehart, Jody, and Gordon and Becki West. *The Discipline Guide,* Loveland, CO: Group Publishing, 1997.

Collins, Marva, and Civia Tamarkin. *The Marva Collins Way*. Charlottesville, VA: Hampton Roads Publishing Co, 1992.

Dobson, James. *Dare to Discipline*. Carol Stream, IL: Tyndale House Publishers, 2004.

Dreikurs, Rudolph. *Maintaining Sanity in the Classroom*. New York, NY: Taylor and Francis, 1998.

Dreikurs-Furguson, Eva, and Pearl Cassels. *Discipline Without Tears*. Rev. ed. Hoboken, N.J: Wiley Publishing, 2004.

Garbarino, J. *Lost Boys*. New York, NY: The Free Press, 1999.

Gibbs, Ollie E., and Jerry Haddock. *Classroom Discipline*. Colorado Springs, CO: Association of Christian Schools International, 1995.

Ginnot, H., and Wallace Goddard. *Between Teacher and Child*. New York, NY: A Three Rivers Press Book, Random House, 2003.

Glasser, William. *The Quality School: Managing Students Without Coercion*. Rev. ed. New York, NY: Harper Perennial, 1998.

Jones, Fredric H. *Positive Classroom Discipline*. New York, NY: McGraw Hill, 1987.

Lightfoot, Sarah Lawrence. *The Good High School: Portraits of Character and Culture*. New York, NY: Basic Books, 1985.

Lipsitz, Joan. *Successful Schools for Young Adolescents*. New Brunswick, NJ: Transaction Books, 1994.

Perretti, Frank. *Wounded Spirit*. Nashville, TN: W. Publishing Group, 2000.

Warren, Paul, and Jody Capehart. *Marching to the Beat of A Different Drum*. Dallas, TX: Sampson Educational Resources, 2003.

LEARNING STYLES

Armstrong, Thomas. *In Their Own Way*. New York, NY: St. Martin's Press, 1987.

Armstrong. *Multiple Intelligences in the Classroom*. Alexandria, VA: Association for Supervision and Curriculum Development, 1994.

Armstrong. *Seven Kinds of Smart*. New York, NY: Penguin Books, 1993.

Butler, Kathleen A. *It's All in Your Mind*. Columbia, CT: The Learner's Dimension, 1988.

Capehart, Jody. *Cherishing and Challenging Your Children*. Wheaton, IL: Victor Books, 1991.

Capehart, Jody, and Gordon and Becki West. *The Discipline Guide for Children's Ministry*. Loveland, CO: Group Publishing, Inc., 1997.

Capehart, Jody, and Paul Warren. *You and Your ADD Child*. Nashville, TN: Thomas Nelson Publishers, 1995.

Carbo, Marie, Rita Dunn, and Kenneth Dunn. *Teaching Students to Read Through Their Individual Learning Styles*. Reston, VA: Reston Publishing Co., Inc., 1986.

Dobson, James. *Dare to Discipline*. Wheaton, IL: Tyndale House Publishers, 1991.

Dobson. *The New Strong-Willed Child: Birth Through Adolescence*. Wheaton, IL: Tyndale House Publishers, 2004.

Dryden, Gordon, and Jeannette Vos. *The Learning Revolution*. Rolling Hills Estates, CA: Jalmar Press, 1994.

Dunn, Kenneth, and Rita Dunn. *Practical Approaches to Individualizing Instruction*. West Nyack, NY: Parker Publishing Co., Inc., 1972.

Dunn, Rita, and Kenneth Dunn. *Teaching Students Through Their Individual Learning Styles*. Reston, VA: Reston Publishing Co., Inc.

Dunn, Rita, Kenneth Dunn, and Donald Treffinger. *Bringing Out the Giftedness in Your Child*. New York, NY: John Wiley and Sons, Inc., 1992.

Dunn, Rita, and Shirley Griggs. *Learning Styles: Quiet Revolution in American Secondary Schools*. Reston, VA: National Association of Secondary School Principals, 1988.

Freudenburg, Ben, with Rick Lawrence. *The Family-Friendly Church*. Loveland, CO: Group Publishing, Inc., 1998.

Fuller, Cheri. *Home Life*. Tulsa, OK: Honor Books, 1988.

Fuller. *Unlocking Your Child's Learning Potential*. Colorado Springs, CO: Piñon Press, 1994.

Gardner, Howard. *The Unschooled Mind: How Children Think and How Schools Should Teach*. New York, NY: Harper Collins Publishers, Inc., 1991.

Gilbert, Anne Green. *Teaching the Three R's Through Movement Experiences*. New York, NY: Macmillam Publishing Co., 1977.

Goleman, Daniel. *Emotional Intelligence*. New York, NY: Bantam Books, 1995.

Gregorc, Anthony. *An Adult's Guide to Style*. Columbia, CT: Gregorc Associates Inc., 1982.

Hannaford, Carla. *The Dominance Factor: How Knowing Your Dominant Eye, Ear Brain, Hand and Foot Can Improve Your Learning*. Arlington, VA: Great Ocean Publishers, 1997.

Kohn, Alfie. *No Contest*. New York, NY: Bantam Books, 1995.

Kolb, David A. *Experiential Learning*. Englewood Cliffs, NJ: Prentice-Hall, Inc. 1983.

Lawrence, Gordon. *People Types and Tiger Stripes*. Gainesville, FL: Center to Applications of Psychological Type, Inc., 1993.

LeFever, Marlene D. Learning Styles: *Reaching Everyone God Gave You to Teach*. Colorado Springs, CO: David C. Cook Publishing Co., 1995.

Leffert, Nancy, Peter L. Benson, and Jolene L. Roehlkepartain. *Starting Out Right: Developmental Assets for Children*. Minneapolis, MN: Search Institute, 1997.

Kotulak, Ronald. *Inside the Brain*. Kansas City, MO: Andrews and McMeel, 1997.

Martin, Grant. *The Hyperactive Child*. Wheaton, IL: Victor Books, 1992.

McCombs, Barbara L., and Jo Sue Whisler. *The Learner-Centered Classroom and School*. San Francisco, CA: Jossey-Bass Inc., 1997.

McDowell, Josh, and Bob Hostetler. *Right From Wrong*. Dallas, TX: Word, Inc., 1994.

Nash, Madeleine. "Fertile Minds." *Time Magazine,* Feb. 3, 1997, pp. 48-56.

Rohm, Dr. Robert. *Positive Personality Insights*. Columbus, GA: Brentwood Christian Press, 1992.

Rose, Colin, and Malcolm J. Niholl. *Accelerated Learning for the 21st Century*. New York, NY: Delacorte Press, 1997.

Sayers, Dorothy. Lecture: "The Lost Tools of Learning." New York, NY: National Review, 1947.

Schindler, Claude E., Fr., with Pacheco Pyle. *Sowing for Excellence: Educating God's Way*. Whittier, CA: Association of Christian Schools International, 1987.

Sousa, Dr. David A. *How the Brain Learns*. Reston, VA: National Association of Secondary School Principals, 1995.

Stevens, Suzanne H. *Classroom Successes for the LD and ADHD Child*. Winston-Salem, NC: John F. Blair, 1997.

Sweet, Leonard. Eleven Genetic *Gateways to Spiritual Awakening,* Nashville, TN: Abingdon Press, 1998.

Swindoll, Charles R. You and Your Child: *A Biblical Guide for Nurturing Confident Children From Infancy to Independence*. Colorado Springs, CO: Focus on the Family, 1994.

Tobias, Cynthis. *Every Child Can Succeed*. Colorado Springs, CO: Focus on the Family, 1994.

Voges, Ken, and Ron Braund. *Understanding Why Others Misunderstand You.* Chicago, IL: Moody Press, Inc., 1994.

Warden, Michael D. *Extraordinary Results From Ordinary Teachers.* Loveland, CO: Group Publishing, Inc., 1998.

Wilson, Douglas. *Recovering the Lost Tools of Learning: An Approach to Distinctively Christian Education.* Wheaton, IL: Crossway Books, 1991.

Wilson, Douglas, Wesley Callihan, and Douglas Jones. *Classical Education and the Home School.* Moscow, ID: Canon Press, 1995.

Zacharias, Raye. *Styles and Profiles.* 1215 Whispering Lane, Southlake, Texas 76092.

Zuck, Roy B. *Teaching as Jesus Taught.* Grand Rapids, MI: Baker Books, 1995.

LEARNING STYLE RESOURCES

Carbo, Dr. Marie. "Reading Style Inventory." National Reading Styles Institute, Box 39, Syosset, NY 11791.

Dunn, Rita. "Learning Styles Network and Resources." Center for Study of Learning and Teaching Styles, St. John's University, Grand Central and Utopia Parkways, Jamaica, NY 11439.

McCarthy, Bernice. "The 4MAT System." EXCEL, 200 West Station Street, Barrington, IL 60010.

MUSIC

Brentwood Music Publishing, Inc., One Maryland Farms, Suite 200, Brentwood, TN 37027.

The Donut Man, Rob Evans, 247 Bay Shore, Hendersonville, TN 37015.

For Kids Only, P.O. Box 10237, Newport Beach, CA 92658.

G.T. Halo Express (Bible Verses to Music), 1987 King Communications, P.O. Box 24472, Minneapolis, MN 55424.

Integrity Music, 1000 Cody Road, Mobile, AL 36695.

Kids for Kids, Barry McGuire, 5490 E. Butler Avenue, Fresno, CA 93727.

Maranatha, P.O. Box 1396, Costa Mesa, CA 92626.

Mary Rice Hopkins, P.O. Box 362, Montrose, CA 91021.

Motions 'n Music, Scripture Press Publications, Inc., 1825 College Avenue, Wheaton, IL 60187.

Psalty Tapes, Word, Inc., 5221 N. O'Conner Blvd., Suite 1000, Irving, TX 75039.

Salvation Songs for Children, Child Evangelism Fellowship, 2300 E. Highway M, Warrenton, MO 63383.

Sing a Song of Scripture, Lillenas Publications, Kansas City, MO 64141.

MULTIPLE INTELLIGENCES

Armstrong, Thomas. *Awakening Your Child's Natural Genius: Enhancing Curiosity, Creativity, and Learning Ability.* New York, NY: The Putnam Publishing Group, 1991.

Armstrong. *In Their Own Way: Discovering and Encouraging Your Child's Personal Learning Style.* Los Angeles, CA: Jeremy P. Tarcher, Inc., 1987.

Armstrong. *Multiple Intelligences in the Classroom.* Alexandria, VA: Association for Supervision and Curriculum Development, 1994.

Armstrong. *7 Kinds of Smart: Identifying and Developing Your Many Intelligences.* New York, NY: Plume, Penguin Group, 1993.

Bates, D., and D. Keirsey. *Please Understand Me: Character and Temperament Types.* CA: Prometheus Nemesis Book Company, 1984.

Bellanca, J., and R. Fogarty. *Multiple Intelligences: A Collection.* Platine, IL: IRI/Skylight Publishing, 1995.

Bruetsch, Anne. *Multiple Intelligences Lesson Plan Book*. Tucson, AZ: Zephyr Press,1995.

Callahan-Young, S., and Anna T. O'Connor. *Seven Windows to a Child's World: 100 Ideas for the Multiple Intelligences Classroom*. Platine, IL: IRI/ Skylight Publishing, 1994.

Campbell, Bruce. *The Multiple Intelligences Handbook: Lesson Plans and More*. Stanwood, WA: Campbell and Assoc, 1994.

Campbell, B., and D. Dickinson. *Teaching and Learning Through Multiple Intelligences*. Stanwood, WA: New Horizons for Learning, 1992.

Chapman, Carolyn. *If the Shoe Fits: How to Develop Multiple Intelligences in the Classroom*. Platine, IL: IRI/Skylight Publishing, 1993.

Gardner, Howard. *Creating Minds*. New York, NY: BasicBooks, HarperCollins Publishers, 1993.

Gardner, Howard. *Frames of Mind: The Theory of Multiple Intelligences*. New York, NY: BasicBooks, HarperCollins Publishers, 1985.

Gardner. *Multiple Intelligences: The Theory in Practice*. New York, NY: BasicBooks, HarperCollins Publishers, 1993.

Gardner. *The Unschooled Mind: How Children Think and How Schools Should Teach*.New York, NY: BasicBooks, 1991.

Goleman, Daniel. *Emotional Intelligence*. New York, NY: Bantam Books, 1995.

Haggerty, Brian. *Nurturing Intelligences: A Guide to Multiple Intelligences Theory and Teaching*. California Innovative Learning, Addison-Wesley Publishing Company, 1995.

Jorgensen, G., and B. Wood. *A Treasure Chest for Teachers and Children Too: Themes to Foster Multiple Intelligences*. Dalby, Queensland, Australia: Heads Together (available through Zephyr Press), 1994.

Kovalik, Susan. *ITI: The Mode—Integrated Thematic Instruction*. Covington, WA: Books for Educators, 1993.

Lazear, David. *Multiple Intelligences Approaches to Assessment: Solving the Assessment Conundrum*. Tucson, AZ: Zephyr Press, 1994.

Lazear, David. *Seven Pathways of Learning: Teaching Students and Parents About Multiple Intelligences*. Tucson, AZ: Zephyr Press, 1994.

Lazear. *Seven Ways of Teaching: The Artistry of Teaching With Multiple Intelligences*. IL: Skylight Publishing, 1991.

Margulies, Nancy. *The Magic 7: Tools for Building Your Multiple Intelligences*. (Interactive Comics, Vol. 2) Tucson, AZ: Zephyr Press, 1995.

Routman, Regie. *Invitations: Changing as Teachers and Learners K-12*. Toronto, Canada: Irwin Publishing, 1991.

Walker, Rena. *Accelerating Literacy: A Handbook to Assist Educators in Creating Balanced Literacy Instruction*. San Diego, CA: Walker Enterprises, 1995.

PRAYER

Avila, St. Theresa. *A Life of Prayer*. Portland, OR: Multnomah Press, 1972.

Bounds, E.M. *Power Through Prayer*. Grand Rapids, MI: Baker Book House, 1972.

Christenson, Evelyn. *Lord, Change Me*. Wheaton, IL: Victor Books, 1979.

Christenson. *What Happens When Women Pray*. Wheaton, IL: Victor Books, 1975.

Foster, Richard J. *Celebration of Discipline: The Path to Spiritual Growth (Rev. ed)*. San Francisco, CA: Harper and Row, 1988.

Getz, Gene A. *Praying for One Another*. Wheaton, IL: Victor Books, 1989.

Gofforth, Rosalind. *How I Know God Answers Prayers*. Chicago, IL: Back to the Bible Publishers, Moody Press, 1983.

Marshall, Catherine. *Adventures in Prayer*. Old Tappan, NJ: Spire Books, 1975.

Mitchell, Curtis, C. *Praying Jesus' Way*. Old Tappan, NJ: Fleming H. Revell, 1946.

Murray, Andrew. *With Christ in the School of Prayer.* Westwood, NJ: Fleming H. Revell, 1972.

Torrey, R.A. *How We Pray.* Chicago: Moody Press, 1989.

REFERENCE BOOKS

Alexander, David, and Pat Alexander, editors. *Eerdman's Handbook to the Bible.* Grand Rapids, MI: William B. Eerdmans Publishing Co., 1973.

Beers, V. Gilbert. *The Victor Handbook of Bible Knowledge.* Wheaton, IL: Victor Books, 1981.

Gangel, Kenneth O., Howard G. Hendricks, and the Dallas Theological Seminary Christian Education Faculty. *The Christian Educator's Handbook on Teaching.* Wheaton, IL: Victor Books, 1980.

Richards, Lawrence O. *The Teacher's Commentary.* Wheaton, IL: Victor Books, 1987.

Walvoord, John F., and Roy B. Zuck. *The Bible Knowledge Commentary.* Wheaton, IL: Victor Books, 1985.

Wright, Fred H. *Manners and Customs of Bible Lands.* Chicago, IL: Moody Press, 1953.

RESOURCES FOR "DOERS"

Books

Bolinsky, Mike. *Affirmative Guide to Creative Bible Teaching.* P.O. Box 833, Cedar Hills, Texas 75104.

Cavalletti, Sofia. *The Religious Potential of the Child.* Ramsey, NJ: Paulist Press, 1979.

Gettman, David. *Basic Montessori Learning Activities for Under Fives.* New York, NY: St. Martin's Press, 1987.

Montessori, Maria. *The Absorbent Mind.* New York, NY: Delta Books, Dell Publishing Co., 1980.

Montessori. *Childhood Education.* New York, NY: A Meridian Book, 1955.

Montessori. *The Montessori Methods.* New York, NY: Schocken Books, 1964.

Montessori. *The Secret of Childhood.* New York, NY: Ballentine Books: The Random House Publishing Group, 1966.

Companies and Organizations

Association of Christian Schools International, P.O. Box 35097, Colorado Springs: CO 80935.

Betty Lukens, Felt Books and Products, P.O. Box 1007, Rohnert Park, CA 94928.

Bible in Living Sound, P.O. Box 234, Norland, WA 98358.

Carraway Street, Inc., Ron Solomon, 200 Frontier City, Chanhassen, MN 55317.

Child Evangelism Fellowship Press, P.O. Box 348, Warrenton, MO 63383.

Christian Educators' Association International, 1550 E. Elizabeth St. Pasadena, CA 91104.

Comics in the Classroom: A Learning Styles Approach. Canadian Daily Newspaper Publishers Association, 890 Yonge Street, #1100, Toronto, Ontario M4W EP.

Cornerstone Curriculum Project, 2006 Flatcreek, Richardson, TX 75080.

Creative Children's Ministries, 7427 Orangethorpe Suite I, Buena Park, CA 90621.

Creative Teachers Publications—Task Cards for Reading, P.O. Box 41, Willstone Park, NY 11596.

Judy Instructor Puzzles, Minneapolis, MN 55406. (Also Available from Shining Star Publications.)

KONOS Character Curriculum, P.O. Box 1534, Richardson, TX 75083.

Learning Research Associates, Inc., P.O. Box 349, Dept. 6, Roslyn Heights, NY 11596.

Little Christian Supply (for ages 1-3), P.O. Box 1763, Blytheville, AR 72316-1763.

Marcy Cook Math Materials, P.O. Box 5840, Balboa Island, CA 92662.

Mortensen Math, P.O. BOX 763068, Dallas, TX 75376.

National Reading Styles Institute, P.O. Box 39, Roslyn Heights, NY 11577.

NavPress Publishing Group, The Navigators, P.O. Box 6000, Colorado Springs, CO 80934.

One Way Street, Inc., P.O. Box 2398, Littleton, CO 80101.

The Perfection Form Company (Reading Beyond the Basics for primary grades and Portals to Reading for intermediate grades), 1000 North Second Avenue, Logan, IA 51546.

Play 'N Talk, 7105 Manzanita Street, Carlsbad, CA 92009.

Sing Spell Read and Write, CBN Center, Virginia Beach, VA 23463.

Sound Reading Associates, Sharon Briggs and Ginny Sorrell, 13704 Springstone Court, Clifton, VA 22024.

Sponge Activities, Idea Factory, 275 East Pleasant Valley Road, Camarillo, CA 93010.

Writing To Think and Thinking to Write, 85 Main Street, Watertown, MA 02172.

SPECIAL NEEDS

Joni and Friends, P.O. Box 3333, Agoura Hills, CA 91301.

Pierson, Jim. *Exceptional Teaching.* Cincinnati, OH: Standard Publishing, 2002.

Pierson. *No Disabled Souls.* Cincinnati, OH: Standard Publishing, 1998.

TEACHER TRAINING

Alley, Steve. *Growing a Healthy Children's Ministry.* Cincinnati, OH: Standard Publishing, 2002.

Child Evangelism Fellowship, 2300 E. Highway M. Warrenton, MO 63383-3420.

James, Steven. *The Creative Storytelling Guide for Children's Ministry.* Cincinnati, OH: Standard Publishing, 2002.